THE POWER TO DISCOVER LIMITLESS
POTENTIAL IN EVERYDAY LIFE

INFINITE YOU

JEANETTE PETERSON

First published by Ultimate World Publishing 2022
Copyright © 2022 Jeanette Peterson

ISBN

Paperback: 978-1-922828-16-3
Ebook: 978-1-922828-17-0

Jeanette Peterson has asserted her rights under the Copyright, Designs and Patents Act 1988 to be identified as the author of this work. The information in this book is based on the author's experiences and opinions. The publisher specifically disclaims responsibility for any adverse consequences which may result from use of the information contained herein. Permission to use information has been sought by the author. Any breaches will be rectified in further editions of the book.

All rights reserved. No part of this publication may be reproduced, stored in or introduced into a retrieval system, or transmitted in any form, or by any means (electronic, mechanical, photocopying, recording or otherwise) without the prior written permission of the author. Any person who does any unauthorised act in relation to this publication may be liable to criminal prosecution and civil claims for damages. Enquiries should be made through the publisher.

Cover design: Ultimate World Publishing
Layout and typesetting: Ultimate World Publishing
Editor: Alex Floyd-Douglass
Front Cover Image: David Nightingale Photography
Back Author Image: Westend Photography

Ultimate World Publishing
Diamond Creek,
Victoria Australia 3089
www.writeabook.com.au

TESTIMONIALS

∞

"Love the style and content Jeanette. It's direct yet soothing and it feels like a comforting blanket on a cold winter's night. I feel like grabbing a cuppa and settling in for a good read. Bravo!"

**Justin Cooper, Author,
Coach and Owner of Brand Purpose Co.**

"Jeanette has penned a wonderful book that instantly draws you in because it's written from the heart. Her insight and practical techniques are unique and helpful guidance through things that hold us back from being as happy and successful as we all deserve to be – whether it's overcoming small roadblocks or major life experiences. The book takes you to times and places that may not always feel comfortable, but I immediately trusted in Jeanette, because she bares her soul, sharing some of her own painful and personal experiences, the effect they've had and how she's been able to move through them to be in a great space today. If you're ready to make happy changes in your life, I highly recommend her wonderful book."

Simon Hillier, Web Content Writer and Trainer

"Reading this book is like having a conversation with a dear friend who cares deeply about this world and everyone in it. Jeanette holds the reader gently in her words of love and encouragement as she peels back the layers of her own growth journey. She unveils life in its full glory, sharing generously and honestly, without sugar-coating the bitter bits. This is a book about hope and the power of love for self – a beautiful gift for everyone who is blessed to meet it."

Joanne Sofia Chong, Optimist

"Across a bright and heartfelt narration, Jeanette helps to uncover incredible potential in you to radically improve your dull life. The book is an effective step-by-step guidance to take control of your existence back from the burden of the past."

Oleg Boukhavlov, Enterprise Evolution Strategist

"Jeanette was born with the natural gift of healing others. She has the innate ability to feel and understand the blockages people are experiencing and use the tools she has learned throughout her life to help heal naturally and effectively. Her writing is seamless and so easy to read that you won't want to put the book down. She courageously delves into topics that most wouldn't dare, and yet speaks so openly and effortlessly you're sure to find an ability to apply learnings into your own life. I recommend this book to anyone on the journey of self discovery."

Jay Marquardt, Day Trader, Warrior Trading

DEDICATION
∞

To all the amazing people who have lifted my spirits and held space for me in your hearts through my darkest moments and my greatest joys; I honour you all, humbled by your presence in my life, each moment of every day.

And, of course, my faithful dog and wise companion, Scooter, who sat diligently by my side every step of the way through my journey until you continued on your own journey over the rainbow bridge.

I dedicate this book to my Dearest mother I simply called 'Ma', who passed away during the writing of this book. At the time, she was my greatest supporter and my biggest critic all at once. For that, I will be eternally both humbled and incredibly grateful.

CONTENTS

Preface		ix
Introduction		1
Chapter 1:	The defining moment	5
Chapter 2:	A journey of 427 days	17
Chapter 3:	Finding The yogi in us all	31
Chapter 4:	Is your pain a superpower?	37
Chapter 5:	In the beginning	43
Chapter 6:	The principles of unboxing	49
Chapter 7:	Get unpacking	71
Chapter 8:	The significance of dreams	77
Chapter 9:	The world of boxes	83
Chapter 10:	The death boxes	91
Chapter 11:	The need for humour	103
Chapter 12:	Find your tribe	109
Chapter 13:	Share your story	119
Chapter 14:	Catch yourself in the act	129
Chapter 15:	Living on the edge	133
Chapter 16:	The curve of contentment	139
Chapter 17:	Infinite you	149
About the author		155
Acknowledgements		157
Connect with me		159

PREFACE
∞

In writing this book, I intend to gently take you on a familiar journey where you might discover how to feel into the depth of the twists and turns as I did – both experiencing and writing it – with the expressed view to share the wisdom I have gained with you.

Give yourself permission to look within as you journey through these pages.

Let whatever rises come to the surface and embrace it into your life. Welcome every feeling and begin to expand as you learn, grow and understand yourself better.

This book seeks to provoke a journey of self-discovery. One that may very well lead you on the most beautiful journey you have yet experienced in life.

It is your journey of authenticity to uncover your infinite potential, which is there for the taking. It has been here within you all along waiting for you to see.

So, step into your vulnerability and join me in this beautiful place where I share some very personal experiences that may help you to both remember and embrace all of those experiences in life that have made you who you are today.

INFINITE YOU

Take your time, make notes, pause and come back again as many times as it takes to find your way home. The beautiful home that resides within you; to where your pure essence exists. Your purpose and understanding exist here to deliver you to your best life possible – filled with wonder, joy and valuable lessons as you step along the path we have come to call life.

And, one more thing before we get started: remember I am here with you every step of the way.

INTRODUCTION
∞

People have often asked me how I can be so positive in a world where so much often feels like its going wrong. The answer is more simple than you might think at first.

Positivity is a state of mind.

It is not something fabricated or put on. My positivity exists within me because I am self-driven to do good in the world. I have chosen to show up in the world authentically. I have learned that as a woman, I am far more powerful when I show up in the world authentically, and at my least powerful when I do not. Therefore, the positivity that people see in me is simply authenticity shining from the inside out. It is the simple found within the complexity.

I have long lost the desire to seek love externally. On the journey of life, I have chosen within my heart to become that which I sought for so long – for I am within myself, love itself. When I chose this path, love chose me at every turn and in every corner of my life, love flows infinitely.

I am sharing my personal story of courage, perseverance and triumph, so that you too can find the light on inside and radiate your authenticity out to the world. To radiate your possibility from within to others is incredibly powerful.

INFINITE YOU

Rather than being drowned out by the noise outside, go within and discover a beautiful new world. You will discover the person you were always meant to be. In doing this, you act as a beacon of light and strength, to give others permission to do the same. Just as others were the beacon of light for me, I am now passing on the lantern. There is much to do, but remember, it is not a race to the finish line.

The outside world is filled with noise and distraction. However, there is infinite potential inside you, and it is all there for the taking. You, and only you, have the manual for your life – but you will not find it searching endlessly outside.

This book might help you to find your manual and start radiating – then, once your light is on, your tribe will be looking for you. Like a beautiful story, if you're brave and keep an open heart, you will find your tribe because they are, in fact, searching for you, too.

So, I say to you, go in and find your light, and switch it on please. Many people are walking around in the dark waiting for your light to shine on them. After all, only lightness can fill the dark.

In this new world filled with disruption, there appears to be much darkness – however, as you journey within, you will discover the potential of unlimited light, just as I have.

My recollection of a story I was told as a child was about an unknown great Indian Chief who once said:

> "Two wolves are fighting inside you, one is the darkness and one is light, one is full of fear, anger and hatred and the other is full of love humility and integrity. The child says to the wise Chief which wolf will win and the Chief says to the child whichever you decide to feed." (Author Unknown)

INTRODUCTION

The question for you each day of your life is, which wolf are you feeding?

Feed the wolf of love, humility and integrity and you will be living a life driven by purpose. This purpose will bring great joy into your life. You will encourage the very same joy into the lives of others as you uncover your authenticity buried below the surface.

As you continue to read, you may laugh, and you may cry, but you may also find just enough courage to start your journey. I am being vulnerable so that you can step into my light and be vulnerable, too.

I will hold space for you just as others have done for me.

I remember some very special words that I was once told from a friend. They meant very little in the beginning but became profound to me on my journey, and remain with me always.

> *"You have never been more ready for this moment on this day right now than you have ever been in your life before today. It is most certainly your greatest truth and your time to shine. (Author Unknown)*

Move forward on your journey to discover the infinite you through the power of going inside when everyone else is looking outside. Here, lies your infinite potential. But first, you must stop looking for it on someone else's path.

It is time to cut your own path, for that is where your true purpose in life, will be revealed in all its glory. It will be the greatest and most important journey you will ever embark on; your journey of self-discovery.

INFINITE YOU

Your recipe for success is simple.

Remain open no matter what comes up, reflect and learn from all experiences and keep moving forward – no matter how tough or enjoyable the road gets. The road is long as there is no beginning and there is no end.

> Are you ready to embark on this journey together?

CHAPTER 1

THE DEFINING MOMENT

Don't let your past define you, be courageous and you never know where life might just surprise you and give you your defining moments in the light.

Not so long ago on a cold, wintery Melbourne day, I had the pleasure of sitting in a room with a group of 33 incredible people. These people, including myself, had decided to take a significant leap of faith and step into the unknown. This gathering was not by chance a life-changing experience – for everyone in the room.

It was day one of a three-day intensive speakers course and our world as we knew it was about to change forever.

As we all entered the conference room in the hotel, most of us were apprehensive and nervous about where we were heading. Had we made a terrible mistake and wasted our money or were our lives about to be transformed forever?

I had been looking forward to this very day for more than a year. With a strong memory that seemed like it was just yesterday, it sat clear in my mind as to why I had chosen to attend. I had felt a sense of calling to be in the speaking space for many years and attended many seminars to find my place. Time and time again, I did not find what I was looking for, so I walked away. But this day was different, and I had also found some more of my tribe.

It was nearly nine o'clock in the morning, and I was both what seemed like excited and nervous at the same time. As science tells us, nervousness and excitement are simply the same things to the body right, with just a differed tilt in our mind. Tell that to my body. It would seem I was shitting bricks and apparently, it showed.

I took my seat – in the front row, of course – and I found myself as if by sheer magic, sitting next to a lovely kind-hearted person who introduced herself to me. The universe had indeed been kind and placed her right by my side. The significance of this moment was not immediately apparent, but over the next three days, I became increasingly more aware that our lives had collided for a reason. I was touched by the beauty – not of coincidence but destiny.

As we began, I remember uttering the words of a dear friend, more than a year before, *"You have got this, keep going."*

To this day, I find myself saying these words each time I need to take a deep breath, back myself and step up. It has not always been easy, but the best things in life usually are not, are they? I was growing more accustomed to the discomfort that is required for growth, more so than at any time in my life previously.

After three days of stepping up, again and again, being courageous and finding myself, in sometimes what seemed the dark, I not only survived. I flourished. I had some incredible moments during those three days that took me to places that both scared me and

THE DEFINING MOMENT

exhilarated me in ways I had never thought imaginable. I re-learned that diamonds are ever so graciously made under pressure.

In my life, I have become accustomed to pressure on numerous occasions. In many of these times, they were pressures I put on myself to perform at my best in a desire to achieve perfection. Over many years of suffering and torturing myself, I discovered that the idea of perfection is merely a figment of our imagination. Perfection, however, does not exist. What appears perfect at this moment is imperfect in the next and vice versa. The striving for perfection in life seems like an endless road that never leads to anywhere.

> Is this sounding familiar to you?

On day two, came one of many defining moments I have experienced in my life. Of course, my beautiful new friends were there holding space, like a gift from the heavens. During the day, we had participated in a group session supporting each other. We were all incredibly tired, but we pushed on.

I was stuck somehow on my why, and someone gave it a gentle prod. It felt uncomfortable like she has made an incision into an already tired and weary body, but with my re-discovered child like curiosity, I was determined to stick with it, feel and see where it took me.

When the day of the training ended, it was time to eat and return to the hotel. Another defining moment came at dinner, right in the middle of a Japanese restaurant on a busy Saturday night.

INFINITE YOU

Yes, like most, I have always been one to prefer my breakthrough moments to happen in quiet, contemplative ways at home. However, anyone who has had a big breakthrough moment in life knows they invariably do not happen that way at all. The biggest and best are usually what one considers potentially embarrassing at the time, and often even immediately after on reflection.

Picture it: me, a grown woman blubbering her eyes out, in the middle of a beautiful Japanese restaurant, out of the blue, for what seemed like no apparent reason. Then, moments later I was laughing and joking.

It was as though what had happened during the day, had caused a slight incision in my skin and somehow wanted to open further. I was tired but determined to get to it.

"Let us go and get some dinner," my new friend said. Not realising why I could not get to my why, she did the kindest thing a person can ever do. She gently increased the size of the incision and then so beautifully just held space for me.

She gently poked inside but, still, I could not find my why. The funny thing is what happened next. My beautiful friend simply said, *"Do not worry about it. Let us eat, and it will come to you."*

So eat and laugh we did, enjoying a truly lovely meal. Then, I went back to my hotel, and the magic happened as I slept. I know now that what I had actually done in that moment was to surrender to the natural phenomenon of flow.

As humans, we seem to have a desire to have all the answers immediately when we ask them, but sometimes it is necessary to

THE DEFINING MOMENT

consider it and then just let it sit. I know I am no stranger, as many of us are for overthinking things, but this time, I was determined to let it take its course.

I woke up early the next day and as if by magic, exactly what I needed had arrived. Trust in the big magic that can happen when you surrender to flow, and you too will gain the rewards that it brings.

The transformation was truly extraordinary, and by the end of day three, I had gained what seemed like 32 new best friends and I was forever changed.

A change that even a week later, as I began to write this book, was hard to fathom.

The next leg of my journey in life had begun. With a newfound sense of direction, I headed off into the world determined to be all I can. For, during these three days I had been heard, and I was no longer invisible. I had changed, surrounded by people who were determined to help me on my way.

I had not only discovered my superpowers, but I had also gotten my mojo back and was ready to take the world by storm.

> Are you personally excited by the idea of discovering your superpowers and learn how you too can live your life out in the open, fully with absolute abandon?

It is not only possible, but a small quiet voice inside you is willing it to happen. That voice, like mine was, might just be drowned out by the noisy world that we live in.

INFINITE YOU

That voice is there for you, too, ever so gently whispering these beautiful words, *"I am here, and I am ready. We have got this."*

If you sit quietly on a still day and listen to the gentle sound from within, you will hear them calling you. If you answer their call each time they speak, your life will change, you will find meaning and remain on your purposeful path as your inner guide leads you forward on your journey.

Don't ever be scared when you find yourself wandering off your path. Don't ever think that you have strayed so far off the path that you will never find your way back. It is never too late to turn back now or make a new path – honestly, I think if you haven't strayed at least once, you haven't lived!

The straying off your current life path is quite possibly the valuable life lessons you need to learn on the way. I say do not treat them as bad judgements or mistakes, but rather beautiful and invaluable lessons to learn. Everything is the path – no wrong ways, no dead ends. The essential ingredient to remember is just keep moving forward, whether that is a tiny step or giant leap. It is all forward motion, even the times in life when humility calls upon you to take what feels like ten steps back to then again take one step forward.

> If you have never felt sad, how would you know what happy feels like? If you have never felt angry, how would you know what calm feels like?

To understand good, you must know bad, just as to understand right you must know wrong. Eventually, you might learn there is

THE DEFINING MOMENT

no good, it is not bad, there is no right, and there is no wrong. It is all just living.

Moment by moment, breath by breath, day by day, year by year.

Your defining moments will happen time and time again, and they will make you the person you are in this very moment. As I did, one by one, weaving the stitches of the beautiful creative tapestry that is your life.

I enjoyed unboxing my past that I had packed away so that I could recall some of the defining moments in my life from years gone by. Feeling into them and understanding the importance they played in building my character was essential to bring me to where I am today.

One of my earliest defining moments I can remember was when I realised as an eight-year-old child, my connection to all living things. My father has surprised my sister, brother and I with a trip to the circus. I was sitting in the stand, and I curiously heard a playful sound of a squealing noise coming from under my seat. I was a curious child, so I bent down and put my head between my knees and there below me was a beautiful, little, pink piglet. I was in awe, amazed and couldn't take my eyes off the piglet.

I immediately wanted to climb down below the seat to sit and play with the piglet, but my father wouldn't let me. I returned to my allocated seat as directed by my father, and I cried. I was always a sensitive child. However, I hid my sensitive side from the view of others, concealing the pain deep within my subconscious.

I knew many years later in my life, just how defining that moment was to me. I began to refuse to eat animals, one by one. I gave my parents such a terrible time at meal times. They were concerned for my health, yet I was more concerned for the health of all others, and that circle of love was expanding at an incredibly fast rate of knots.

I recall my next defining moment around connectedness happened at around the age of twelve. I was told, by my father to collect milk from the freezer in the shed. You see my father used to economise when we went shopping and buy our quota of milk for the entire fortnight and freeze them.

I remember it like it was yesterday. I lifted the lid of the freezer to find tiny skinned bunny rabbits lying right there, whole rabbits just without skin. My dad used to go rabbit shooting and bring them back home to eat. Again I cried, but this time inside in my very own private hell because no one understood. It was another experience of mine now held within, and the imprint it left was a heavy burden to bear alone.

Then finally, when I was 16, I was in the passenger seat while my mum was driving. We were on the freeway, and a truck pulled up beside us filled to the brim with crates with what seemed like hundreds of chickens. I had never noticed them before after all the times I had been in the car on a freeway, but today was different. I looked up, and I saw a chicken whose neck that appeared stuck in the wire door of the crate, and he was dying a slow and terrible death right before my very eyes.

You see, our eyes met and it was as if he was crying out for my help right there and then and I could do nothing but cry. It broke my heart right there on the spot. Another wound that I suffered alone and buried deep in my subconscious. By this time, the imprints were pilling up, and the burden was becoming unbearable.

THE DEFINING MOMENT

All of these moments were boxed away, stored in my subconscious. I was not at all equipped to deal with the pain they brought me, so I tried to hide them. You know, out of sight out of mind, but we all know that is an ideal but not a reality. It was just an elaborate coping mechanism – one that I became a master of, or so I thought. The damage made remained with me for many years, and they had left scars that I would need to tend to as an adult.

Today, we journey forward.

Together, we can make the world a better place, so that everyone has a chance to be heard, to be visible and to be their awesome, most authentic selves living a full life.

Your defining moments, just like mine, are important all along the way to help create who you will become. All that is required is action. Some will make you cry with sadness, some might make you cry with joy and others will make you laugh. They are all equally important and to be cherished because they have made you who you are today.

> So I ask you, what have been your defining moments in life?
>
> Have you, just like I did, hidden them from view?
>
> Are they remaining in your subconscious unresolved?
>
> Were you like me, a child not equipped to work through them, so they left a deep imprint?

Before we continue on this journey together, I suggest that you take some time, start a journal and reflect on your defining moments in your life. They may very well hold the keys right now to unlock your future. How cool would that be?

I'm not going anywhere, so get writing in your journal and come back to continue our journey together when you're ready.

In the beginning, don't be concerned that your memory might be slow to come to the party. You only need one to begin. Once you start on this beautiful journey, the memories of your defining moments will unfold just as they did for me. One by one, your subconscious will bring them forward when you are ready to face them.

Whether you lived a life of fear and anger or love and respect, it is okay for you to feel stuck or lost – or even both. Don't ever feel guilty that you should somehow be grateful because you didn't have a terrible childhood. We can all still get lost on the journey of life and wander far off the road – no matter how giving and loving our circumstances appeared to be as a child.

Today is your opportunity to turn back, hop in the driver seat, take control and start the movement forward to journey forward, gathering the pieces of you that you left behind. All we need to do is begin to move in a forward motion again in life. For everything around us is moving.

Let's get you back behind the wheel, so the forward motion will begin once again, and we'll be on our way, together.

THE DEFINING MOMENT

Remember to enjoy the journey, and that in life, there is motion. Sometimes it's clear, sometimes it's blurry and on occasions, it feels completely chaotic. Embrace it all, like you would your best friend.

When you truly come to understand this, you will know you're winning.

CHAPTER 2

A JOURNEY OF 427 DAYS

Begin with only today in mind, for as you step forward, today's decisions will determine tomorrow's opportunities.

Not so long ago, I hit a wall. I was stuck.

> Have you ever felt stuck? I felt invisible. Have you ever felt invisible?

It was as if there was a dark cloud hanging over my head, and no matter what I did, I was unable to shake it off.

I had a good job and people around me who loved me, but something was missing that I could not put my finger on.

> Have you been there, too?

INFINITE YOU

It's a feeling that attacks so many of us at some point in our lives. It can come from what seems like nowhere and stay for what feels like an eternity.

Some like to call it a midlife crisis. I prefer to call it a storage crisis because that is what happened to me.

I am a child of the 70s. I have lived through the changes in the age of technology. What I discovered is that we seem to be living in a world where we place our happiness in the hands of others; where we constantly seek gratification in the collection of things when they only bring us short-term joy.

The year this book was published, I turned 50. It's an incredible feeling to reach such a milestone in life. I feel incredibly grateful to be able to look back at a full life enriched with so many experiences. Like many, I began as a child who was full of life, only to loose my zest for life on my way through childhood and into adulthood with anxiety and self worth issues.

I went on to experience both joy and sadness, yet I made it through in one piece. In fact, I did better. I learned to thrive beyond the feelings of self doubt, loss and regret. I learned to love myself again, collect the pieces I had lost and embody love in the most beautiful way possible. On reflection, my story is like so many others.

And, guess what? You may very well be one of them!

Science tells us that we are living in a world with an epidemic of low self-esteem. I find this information quite alarming. I imagine you might feel the same in knowing or learning this for the first time. Yet like most things in life, it didn't happen overnight for me, and if you are feeling it, the chances are it's crept up on you, too.

Low self esteem, lack of self love or even self loathing is something that just creeps up on you over time. Once you have reached a tipping point, you know you feel like you have hit rock bottom. It become startlingly obvious, in a sledge hammer kind of way.

> So, we get that it happens and it's a problem, right? But answering the question – how did we get here? – is not so easy, yet it's a pretty important question to consider. How did it all go so wrong on such a big scale?

When we start to reflect back to only 100 years ago, we spent the vast majority of our days gathering the ingredients just so we could eat enough to survive. It's a stark difference to now, don't you think?

We have gadgets for everything, so we now have more time to do the things we love and enjoy and less time growing and preparing food, because we have outsourced all that hard work.

> Why then, do we seem to not have enough time to take care of ourselves and experience the potential happiness that exists inside us all?

> Is it because we are living life on hyperdrive?

INFINITE YOU

We rush from A to B, with our head either regretting the past or thinking about the future – instead of living in the here and now. The more technology finds a way to do more tasks for us the more we seem to busy ourselves with other tasks, which are often meaningless to our personal joy and growth.

This hyper speed of technology advancement isn't looking like it is going to slow down anytime soon. We are on the edge of driverless cars and artificial intelligence is growing at warp speed. We've started to build a meta verse, which in a world where we get lost in endless loops of social media, the concept troubles me deeply. Yet we are rushing down the artificial intelligence path, taking generations with us, with what seems like little to no understanding of future implications.

When I consider all of this, it's really no surprise that I felt overwhelmed, and in one moment, I decided I could simply go no further on this personal trajectory of a meaningless life that lacked all purpose.

I decided to take leap of faith. I reached out for help.

I have to tell you this is something that I was not very good at in the past. At all. I was the kind of person who was everything to everyone. That person who everyone thought had their shit together and who everyone else relied on for support and guidance.

> Are you that person to those around you?

A JOURNEY OF 427 DAYS

I was terrified that if I asked for help that I was somehow weak. I was worried at that time what other people would think. I was a professional businesswoman who many relied on.

I had no time for weakness.

This could have been the beginning of the end but it was, in the most divine way, the beginning of something beautiful.

> Have you been taught that seeking help is a weakness, too?

I was known for my strength of character, and people did not mess with me. I had completely and unknowingly backed myself into a corner. The corner where I had painted myself as the heroine who could do it all, while I was completely falling apart inside.

It was a very bitter pill to swallow; one that I was choking on for some time. Yet no one knew it because I did what I thought best, soldiering on in life with a front bigger than Myer, as my mother would have said. It was my very own private living hell.

Finally, I could cope no longer. When the despair set in night after night – with what seemed like crying myself to sleep with rivers of tears – I had a chance encounter with someone well placed to help me. This person who, as luck would have it, generously and lovingly gave me a safe place without judgement. He held space for me for a very long 427 days to be exact, which was no small gesture of kindness at all.

It was truly a blessing and a significant display of unconditional love.

INFINITE YOU

We met, some would say by chance, but I have come to understand that it wasn't chance at all and he knew this completely. Over time, he became a very dear friend. One of whom I will cherish for the rest of my life. Like the father figure I felt I had dearly missed out on for so very long, he filled a void in my heart and together we commenced a beautiful journey where he guided me forward with his kindness.

Over time, his professional support helped me to uncover and work through so many things in my life that I had hidden in the deepest darkest corner of my subconsciousness.

This beautiful journey of 427 days began with an understanding; a meeting of the minds and hearts, along with an unwritten agreement that we would both commit completely. And so, the journey began.

I met with him for weekly sessions where we delved deeply into my past. So deep that I had forgotten these parts of me existed at all. I was rediscovering things that I had boxed up and packaged away deep inside my subconscious – in a process that can only be described as a superpower of a coping mechanism.

After each session, he would write up extensive notes for me to consider, which were up to 20 pages long some weeks. These notes arrived on Thursday every week for the next 61 weeks. For the first nine weeks, the session notes were wrenching. It would take three rounds at them to simply let the content sink in.

The first time I read the notes, I cried so much I could barely read the words on the page. We were going deep and I was feeling completely exposed and consumed by the vulnerability. This was a whole new Jeanette emerging and it was hard.

A JOURNEY OF 427 DAYS

The second time I read the notes, I would still cry a little but this time I managed to absorb the content better.

Then finally, the third time, I said to myself, *"You've got this."*

Initially, I was filled with a child-like sense of enthusiasm to commence the journey fool-heartedly not knowing what lay ahead. As so many of us know, things usually get worse before they get better, and the first nine weeks were true to form.

Week by week, the burden of what seemed unimaginable to bare got bigger and bigger, until at week nine where I thought I could take no more. It was at this point that I had lunch with a very dear friend.

We sat in a beautiful park near my work. I remember this day vividly. It rained and rained, and in reflection, it was as though the rain was washing away my troubles and the words spoken have remained etched in my mind. I told my beautiful friend that I was feeling overwhelmed. I thought I literally might die if I continued; that I could not take anymore. This was not merely a dramatic moment of seeking sympathy – I was feeling the depths of despair unearthing all I had buried.

In her most beautiful, kind and loving way, she said to me, *"Keep going, you've got this,"* and so I sucked it up, took a deep breath and I did just that.

I have so much gratitude for that conversation of hope that kept me going when times got tough. It was her kindness that touched my heart and I remember it fondly as a defining moment in my life.

It seemed as though over those nine weeks that the entire contents of all my life – including my shame, regret and disappointment – that

INFINITE YOU

I had so carefully packed away deep inside my subconscious, were now spilling out all over the floor. I felt exposed and vulnerable in a way I had never imagined possible. I liken it to the feeling of tipping 20 boxes of Lego that had been meticulously packed up out on the lounge room floor.

It felt messy and completely overwhelming.

It took every ounce of courage I could muster to continue, but I dug deep and kept moving forward. To contextualise the situation, I was in the midst of a significant piece of work, so my professional life was busy. The person I undertook this journey with had told me that soon things would level out and start to fall into place. By week 12, just as he said it would, things started to level out and make sense.

I began to again look forward to the sessions and his weekly notes with tasks for me to undertake. Things started to make a great deal of sense indeed, and I was able to recall details from the weeks prior. Over time, I was able to connect the dots with all that was now tipped out on the proverbial floor. I began to see patterns that I was unable to see prior. It was quite magical when I started to see where things repeated and connected again and again.

You see this amazing thing happens when all your shame, disappointment and regret are pooled together like a lake on the floor, right in front of your very own eyes. I could now see the whole picture and, guess what? It was not remotely as bad as the story I had told myself.

> Have you ever felt so scared to do something it made you feel sick? Or have you ever thought something was just too hard to imagine to tackle?

A JOURNEY OF 427 DAYS

That is until you do it and then you say to yourself, *"Wow, that was not as hard or as scary as I thought, after all!"*

> Hindsight can be a wonderful thing, right?

Consider the concept of childbirth. It is a miraculous thing that a woman can endure, but it is scary, all the same. Then magically after birth, when their beautiful baby finally arrives, it's all seemingly forgotten.

I have never had children, but I marvel at the phenomena of this in the women in my life.

In a short space of time, I was finding myself doing what he suggested to do in the earlier weeks without even realising. By the 16th week, people around me were starting to notice the difference in me and began to ask me what I had done. These people were not just those close to me; they were also my work colleagues.

I was different, and I was looking at the world in a new way.

The lens I was viewing the world through had changed for me completely. Not only was I feeling the shift within me, but now, so were others.

Things were finally starting to fall into place for me, and the dark cloud I had felt overhead had finally, started to disappear. It was a beautiful day I recall – during the 16th week – when I realised that my life had indeed changed forever. It is hard to find words to explain how I felt that day, but I know two things with certainty. I felt a whole lot lighter than I had for a very long time, and I knew my life had changed in a way I could never have imagined possible. All thanks to the generosity and kindness of a stranger.

Never underestimate the power you have to change the life of others with both your kindness and generosity, beyond your inner circle.

As we continued our journey together that lasted a total of 61 life-changing weeks, not only did our relationship gain a depth of trust and mutual respect, but so did my relationships with many people around me.

I began to really open up to the present moment.

It was not just my boxes from my past that had been opened and spilled out onto the floor, but my heart's door to vulnerability was ajar for what seemed like the very first time in my entire life. It felt so unimaginably nice, like stepping into the warmth of the sunshine on the first day of summer. I was renewed, with a sense of knowing I belonged, right where I was right now.

It was a great failing on my part, to not see all the people I had around me, who at the drop of a hat, would have provided me with support and kindness. Instead, I was determined to go through the sufferings of life alone and bare the burden exclusively. I believe this is something that I imagine many reading this story will resonate with. As many will understand that shame or embarrassment too often leaves us to bear our burdens alone, when we need not.

Let me let you in on a little secret...

There are not, nearly eight billion of us here on planet earth for us all to suffer in silence.

A JOURNEY OF 427 DAYS

We are all here to support one another, so never feel alone, because you most certainly are not. There are many people in your life, who are completely ready and waiting to lend a hand, in your time of need. You, simply need to be a little vulnerable, reach out and step out into their light. You, like I was, are sure to find your very own person, waiting to take your hand and hold space for you, so that you too can heal.

This person may be someone you already know or someone you will meet at any moment.

Therefore, it is important to keep your eyes and heart open, so that you recognise when they arrive in your life. Leave the sceptic behind, be guided by your instincts and be open to meeting new people and having new experiences. People arrive in our lives constantly, yet without present moment awareness and the willingness to seek help, we will miss the opportunities that their arrival brings time and time again. It is never too late to begin to open up.

Start today.

Be present with your friends, family, acquaintances, work colleagues and new people – you never know what beautiful gift of generosity and kindness they may be holding for you.

> Are you, like most of us, and find yourself daydreaming about the future, wishing the working week away and reminiscing about a life gone by?

You are not alone.

INFINITE YOU

This is, unfortunately, a common trap that many of us fall into at some point in our lives. It is one where we are not present today. In this state, you are unable to do the work today to set yourself up for the future you want tomorrow. Then weeks, months and years pass by so quickly, and we feel like we have not moved forward at all. We are stuck in the same job, same life and the same cycle of unhappiness.

I am certain there will be some bells ringing for you right now. Like a mouse trapped on a wheel, it is easy to get stuck – in fact, it's even easier to forget how you got there in the first place.

Be brave and begin your journey. It may take 100 days, or it may take 10,000. The duration is unimportant. The only important thing to do today is deciding to start.

Your choices today will determine tomorrow's opportunities.

A lesson that I learned the hard way, as many of us do. One foot in front of the other. Lots of small steps can achieve big changes in your life, just as can lots of tiny destructive habits.

My number one strength is strategic, so I could not help myself but to try to plan the next 20 steps. I have an uncanny way of seeing the road ahead of most people around me, so I have spent a lifetime trying incredibly hard to plan for everything.

Unfortunately, I cannot plan for every possible outcome. Many people, like I did, spend their entire lives planning, but never actually get anything done. I know it sounds depressing, but I am betting this is not too unfamiliar a scenario for many reading this book. When we plan and the time comes to act, fear is usually what holds us back.

A JOURNEY OF 427 DAYS

Let me make it simple for you. There is only one decision that you need to make today.

No need to try and make them all today. As you make the first decision to start your journey to unpacking those boxes from your past, like magic, things start to appear before you like they had not before. It is like you must open the door to a room, step inside, close it behind you and wait. Then, with patience, the door from that room to the next one appears, when it had not appeared before.

Master the art of waiting, making one decision at a time, and you will know you are heading in the right direction. You do not have to believe me, but try it on for size, and the results will surprise you.

See when you wait, sometimes more information comes to hand to enable you to make a better decision. Sometimes, in my life gone-by, people used to tell me to stop procrastinating. But science tells us that the most creative and successful people seem like they procrastinate on the surface. It is simply, giving the creative bubble time to build and burst.

Today, my best ideas come from letting things sit patiently and letting the solutions arrive, rather than chasing it down. This is what is known as the beautiful art of flow. Our chaotic busy lives often make it virtually impossible to step into a flow state, without planning that is.

Flow is a skill I have taught many a client to feel into. There is not one hard and fast rule when it comes to flow, it feels different for us all. For me when I am in flow I am most creative and writing literally feels like it pours from my finger tips onto the keyboard.

When I am overthinking and overplanning, my flow state becomes blocked, and no matter how hard I push, nothing happens. Flow is like the oxygen in your blood moving through you. If you breath gently and let it be, it simply moves exactly as it should. In the most simplest of terms, planning is pushing and flow is allowing. There are times to push, but also times to allow.

Find your balance practicing to plan and allow – when you get there, you will know.

Please do not chase down all your boxes like a mad person determined to unbox everything in a frenzy. When the first box arrives, take a slow deep breath, open it up, and you have begun. Your life is your journey and yours alone. Live it at your speed. It is not a race. It is not a competition. It is just a journey to be lived in each moment, day by day.

Like a flower blooms, let it unfold as it should.

For far too long, we have become impatient with wanting all the answers right now. The answers will come if you learn to wait patiently. I recall a beautiful piece of advice I received during this period of enlightenment, although I cannot remember where it originates from:

> "Patience is not the art of waiting, but the state of mind whilst you wait." (Author Unknown)

> Can you wait? How do you choose to wait? Is there a voice that whispers as you wait or one that yells? Are you aware of this moment as you wait?

Waiting is indeed an art form that may very well change your whole life in ways you never imagined. So like I did, learn to wait patiently. Nurture it and you may find that your patience will set you free.

CHAPTER 3

FINDING THE YOGI IN US ALL

Take the chance to look deep within, you might be surprised by the beauty and happiness that is laying beneath the surface, at your centre.

The journey of 427 days led me onto the next chapter in my life as a modern-day yogi. This journey continues to this day and will beyond, infinitely. Let me reassure you, I am not suggesting that everyone must become a yogi to find their way forward in life. Although, you never know. It might just help you find your superpowers, too.

That unique gift that only you can bring to the world.

A yogi's journey is many things to many people. To me, it is a journey of kindness and forgiveness. Both buzz words of today, yet we seem to like to use them intermittently in our human lives. We choose when to be kind and when to forgive; all driven by the stories in our mind and our social and cultural conditioning.

The stories I told myself were powerful and very believable, and you might relate to many of them. Some, I thought up for myself.

INFINITE YOU

Some formulated during my upbringing, and a few were even driven into me forcibly by others. Our experiences in life from childhood to adulthood impacts us in many ways – some felt immediately, and some lay dormant for years.

This is the potent process of social and cultural conditioning.

I can honestly say that not in a million years did I imagine that I would become a modern-day yogi. It isn't something that most people think about, is it? As I sit here in my office typing these very words, I feel a sense of awe, as to just what is possible when you look beneath the surface.

A yogi indeed, I chuckle. For most, I imagine that conjures up images of a shaved head and a yellow and red robe, or maybe a very religious grey-haired old man with a beard from India. This is simply part of the belief systems that we developed throughout life. In fact, in reality, if you asked a monk or Indian yogi, you would likely be told – as I was – that the path of yoga is for everyone who chooses to follow it, with every one of our own journeys being equally important.

A yogi is simply someone who practices the art of yoga. But we have, as humans do, created an elaborate vision of what we consider a yogi to be, elevating them to a position unattainable in our perceptions. This is what we know as pedastalising others, and we do it a lot in life, sometime as a subconscious means of getting in our own way.

You see, I decided it was time to break that myth for myself because historically, a yogi has almost always been a male. I have never been one to conform, as that would be like walking someone else's path. I have chosen to cut my own path forward in life, and so I am a modern-day female yogi. It is time that the world learned to deal with that because I am here to write a new story, and so too can you.

Like many people in the modern world today, I was bombarded with an equal combination of religion and anti-religion seemingly everywhere I went. People were always happy to share their opinions and experiences, and often not in a kind way either. I had what I don't think was a unique experience in my childhood. One of my parents believed in God, and the other proclaiming it all to be a big lie. As you can imagine, it was somewhat confusing as a child.

However, every problem brings opportunity, so this one took me on a particularly interesting and awakening journey of self-discovery. One that I would recommend to anyone because self-discovery is about seeking knowledge and making up your own mind.

I was determined to understand, so I made friends as a child, with other children from every religion I could find. I wanted to experience and understand every religion I could for myself. I went from church to church and group to group, and I found the same things with just a slight twist. I met people who were supportive, kind, and loving. Yet, when I discussed this with individuals both inside and outside of these groups, I received a lot of judgement.

It surprised me that I saw unity and others saw a difference.

My journey discovering the true essence of yoga helped me to understand and accept life as it is in this moment, that tomorrow could be completely different and that is ok too.

The journey of yoga is a beautiful and personally enriching experience that has brought me both closer to myself and the universe in one magical union. I feel expanded where I now live in a world of infinite possibilities. It is a world that fills me with a child-like enthusiasm for life and has returned my deep sense of connectedness to all life on this planet. I feel a sense of harmony in my life and an ability to face the road ahead with love, curiosity and wonder – rather than fear, sadness and despair.

One of the most delightful things about my journey through yoga is the people I have had the opportunity to meet. Every time I begin another journey of learning, I marvel at the beautiful souls that I meet. I have learned the importance of people in my life and the richness that their interactions brings to all of life, regardless of their viewpoint. It forever brings joy to my heart and a smile on my face to experience the richness of the human spirit in all its variety.

Yoga has taught me some of the most valuable life lessons, and as I continue on my yogic journey, the love in my heart continues to expand infinitely.

It is a personal journey of self-discovery, and it will continue through the rest of this life and beyond, as I continue to unlock the mysteries of my life and discover my superpowers.

It is a journey that you can embark upon at any time, to find your hidden yogi within.

It doesn't mean you need to remove yourself from society, shave your head and don a yellow robe or grow a beard. In fact, in some of the oldest written texts, the original sages of the Upanishads, were sent back to live life amongst the people. To marry and have children whilst passing on their valuable knowledge and wisdom. We all have a part to play and it's important to expand the lens we apply to the world so that we may see our path ahead.

FINDING THE YOGI IN US ALL

Open your heart to the love that exists not externally to you but deep within, for here lies your infinite potential. Call it whatever you like, but everything that you need to live an infinite life exits within you. You simply need to stop looking outside and begin the beautiful journey of looking inward.

Just remember one thing, yoga is not just exercise, it is so much more.

Take a look and you might be surprised at what the yogi within you could bring to life in your every day. A life of infinite potential and understanding, all starting within you and expanding outwards as if the sun itself is radiating from within your very being.

> Now, who doesn't want to feel that amazing?

It is yours to behold because you already have it within you. You just might not have realised it yet. In me, it was where I found and reconnected to the divine love. You can call it God, your soul, the universal oneness. Whatever you like, but it is just a label, after all.

It is not necessary to give it a name, yet if it works for you, name it as you please.

It is simply meant to be felt. It is a beautiful thing to feel the pure love radiate from within your heart.

Sometimes we struggle to simply feel because we are taught through conditioning to rationalise everything within the mind. When you connect with pure unconditional love in your heart, your life will change forever just as mine did. You will begin to see the world differently to how you have before.

Trust in the process because it isn't like a light coming on for everyone. An epiphany can be a slow burn or a moment of instant awareness. Just give it some space in your heart, and it shall come. First, you must send the invitation.

For me personally, my strong heart connection was where my epiphany of love came to be understood. I no longer seek love externally because I understand that I myself on the inside am the embodiment of pure love, as are you. I was taught, just like everyone, that love came with conditions and that it was to be sought externally.

Repeat with me: *"I am love, at my source, I am pure love radiating, I need not seek it or give it away, I simply need to be love itself."*

That, my friend, is the greatest invitation of love.

CHAPTER 4

IS YOUR PAIN A SUPERPOWER?

Imagine if you discovered hidden intertwined in your greatest pain was actually your superpowers, what would your life look like.

Is your pain a superpower? As scary as that might sound, it is most certainly an idea worth pondering, don't you think? This very concept opened my life up in ways I had never imagined. With just a few simple words from a kind person, at the right moment, the layers were ever so effortlessly peeled back, like the skin of an onion.

And there it was, in all its glory.

You see, I discovered that I indeed have superpowers and I found the first one in a place I would never have imagined to look. That's right. I found my superpower intertwined in my suffering.

> How amazing is that?

INFINITE YOU

Your very own superpowers could be hidden from view, in plain sight, beneath all your despair, regret, shame and disappointment. They are, however, much easier than you think to find.

I was so busy thinking I was going crazy that I had not realised that my ability to box up and pack away all my pain, suffering and disappointment for 40 years into individual boxes was indeed, a superpower. Who would have known such a thing? I am talking major superpowers here, not just something simple. I individually packed and labelled boxes for every disappointment, regret, shame and despair I felt for over 40 years.

If you asked as phycologist or a psychiatrist, they would probably tell you that it was a coping mechanism. Fair enough, but I managed to survive for 40 years, with a pretty good life until I ran out of storage. Yep, one day I completely ran out.

Storage, you might say? Ha! Well, it was not just any old storage system I had. It was elaborate, complicated, and it was huge. A complex system where I managed to box up every individual piece of pain, suffering and disappointment that happened in my life and store it away deep in my subconscious mind.

My ability to store away these things in my mind, yet continue to function in my work and private life, has baffled many. I did it with such absolute gusto, that it became quite an art form. It resembled my very own Fort Knox, locked away until I found the fortitude to start unpacking on my journey of 427 days.

Imagine taking 427 days to move. It sounds tiring, does it not?

IS YOUR PAIN A SUPERPOWER?

Well, it was as I unpacked it one box at a time. The expanse of my very own private Fort Knox initially was still really not entirely known at this point, because as I removed each layer of boxes. I seemed to just make room for more to show up in view. They were endless. It's no wonder I ran out of storage room and I was exhausted holding onto all of that stuff.

It kind of explains a lot really; the exhaustion, that is. I got all the warning signs progressively through life. Gut problems, stress, anxiety and finally chronic fatigue, before I sat up and paid attention to what was really going on.

> What might your pain be trying to reveal to you? Could there be some hidden lessons to be uncovered behind the pain? Could uncovering them reveal your superpowers like mine did?

Don't be disheartened at all by the sheer magnitude of my storage. In fact, see it as a beautiful opportunity to discover what lies below the surface. I did, thankfully, feel that I had broken its back so to speak at the end of the 427 days. What are a few boxes between friends, right?

The funny thing is, I figured once I had discovered this amazing superpower to box my suffering and store it away. Surely, it was going to be child's play to unpack it all right?

Not so quick, Jeanette, this job can not be rushed. It takes time, a sense of presence and a safe space to fulfil what seemed like such a mammoth undertaking.

INFINITE YOU

I do not necessarily suggest that you go hard at it for 427 consecutive days solid. Some people grow progressively in increments, while others grow sharply through exponential growth. However, there are times in life when the universe is providing you with an opportunity to grow suddenly. This was one of those moments for me.

The only requirement for you is to commit to beginning your journey. It will take as many days, weeks or months as it needs to for you. You might just have one giant box or you might have hundreds of tiny boxes. We are all unique so embrace your own uniqueness for what it is.

Don't worry if you don't realise at first that you have superpowers. Remember I did not either at first. In reality, I thought I might very well have been going crazy. I did not realise until someone pointed it out to me in these very simple words, *"It's like a superpower to do what you did."*

It is always beautiful when someone brings the lighter to light your candle, so to speak. Wow, I have superpowers, I had not thought of it like that at all. What a difference that a little perspective has on your thoughts.

> What are your superpowers? Where are yours hidden? Do you have your very own Fort Knox, or do you have one giant box that you are dragging behind you, getting heavier and heavier each day?
>
> Whichever it is, your very own superpowers could be within, buried among a lifetime of experience, simply forgotten or hidden from view. That is a pretty exciting concept, don't you think?

IS YOUR PAIN A SUPERPOWER?

There is a beautiful philosophy in Buddhism that I once read that sheds some light on the concept of superpowers hidden within suffering. It resonated with me and I continue to use it to remind me when I hit a wall where I feel resistance. It reminds me that hidden within every problem lies the seed of the solution.

To simplify, to find the solution you must go through the problem, which in yogic terms is commonly known as sitting with your suffering until it becomes your blessing.

The discovery and practice of this can potentially change the way you look at suffering. In fact, it could change the way you look at every problem that you ever encounter in life.

Don't underestimate its power.

I have over my career worked in many fields and in my later professional career I worked in digital transformation. It doesn't get much more succinct in the problem solving space than that. When I learned to embody the seed of solution hidden within the problem, I became happy to have problems to solve, because I now knew where the solution was, even if it was like finding a needle in the haystack. Over time, I got pretty good at letting the seed find me.

When you have a problem, you also have a solution. Think about how this could relate to your work or personal life. We all have problems that come and go, so I'm sure you won't have any trouble testing this one out.

CHAPTER 5

IN THE BEGINNING

Find the place where it all began and start with that box, if you don't know it then back up slowly and you will find it eventually.

Do you recall a traumatic experience in your life that brought you to a screaming halt? You know, one of those events when you felt like you hit a wall and you could see no way around it? Or even worse, when faced with the wall, you literally ran the other way? Or was your demise like mine, slow and progressive? Did it inch its way into your subconscious little by little over many years?

A slow demise is tricky because you do not see it coming at all. It is like the frog in a pan scenario. Not particularly inviting to think about, but just like the frog, we do not consider getting out, because our environment changed around us so slow that we missed all the signposts on the way. They are subtle, and without awareness they are easy for us to miss entirely. That is until you hit rock bottom when it feels like all the walls around you have come crashing down.

This is usually when the reality of the situation has hit home hard.

Either way, it doesn't matter because you can always find your way forward – just as I did – no matter where life has taken you. Never be discouraged if you are in a place that feels dark. I was there too, and I made it out the other side. I did not just make it out the other side, I flourished.

You can also succeed the same way because that is what the universe intends for us all. You are here to live a full life, which includes all the ups and downs on the way.

The lessons we learn on the way teach us the skills to move forward in life – ready just in time for the next experience.

Regardless of how it all began, some boxes containing your trauma, pain, anguish, disappointment and regret; some will be extremely heavy, and some will be quite light. Treat the heavy ones with the care and self-love that they deserve. Heavy boxes are heavy for a reason – observing and respecting this on your journey to unpack will serve you well.

The content, potentially held in the boxes of your subconscious, are interwoven in all parts of you, just like the tape that holds each of them closed. Sometimes, it feels like you pull out hairs when you try to remove the tape and sometimes, it just falls right off. Feel into where you are in the moment, with whatever comes up from each memory held in the boxes of your subconscious. It is not a race to the finish line. Remember, life is a journey. It may have taken you a long time to suppress the stuff you packed away

IN THE BEGINNING

in your subconscious, so be kind as you open up to it and allow it to surface.

I started with the easier boxes that I felt confident I could tackle, and then worked my way forward to the most difficult ones. For us all, it can be entirely different. Some of us find courage easier to muster. Yet some need to scrape the crumbs together with all the strength we have in the beginning. Whatever it looks like today as you begin to tackle unpacking, remember you are always enough.

I can most certainly promise you one thing. Some boxes will hurt and will make you feel like you cannot bear to open them. Be brave in these moments for there are lessons to learn from the process of opening and releasing the content held within them. I used meditation to gently guide me through the tough ones, to help me sit with the contents, gently inviting it back into my space.

Also, it's important to remember that you do not have to work through this process alone. Having someone coach and support you through the unpacking can make the entire process much more comforting and supportive – while bringing fruitful results.

I did not go at it alone. It took a lot for me to seek help because, through cultural and social conditioning, I believed that asking for help was weak.

Asking for help in times of need is not a weakness. In fact, it is a beautiful strength.

When you ever so gently give the memories that have brought you suffering, pain or disappointment in your life a little room to breathe, you can become the conscious observer. In this process, you get to look upon these things as if they belong to someone else. Almost as though you are offering support and advice to your dearest friend. Remember, some of the memories that felt heavy when you packed them up as a child are completely irrational now that you have grown into an adult.

It is a magical thing to be able to sit back and take a peek, with a sense of disconnection allowing you to interpret the contents with fresh eyes, because so often the pain we hide away is from our childhood, at a time when we were incredibly impressionable.

However, as an adult, we are now able to rationalise the content in a completely different way. Which is incredibly valuable in the process of learning the lesson, and letting go of the emotional attachment that you wrapped around it as a child.

Science tells us that every time we recount our memories, our body goes through the same emotions as if we are reliving it exactly again. Just like at the moment that it occurred the very first time.

What a powerful thing the mind is.

If you remember the beautiful memories of your life, you will feel the warmth in your heart that you felt that very day. Likewise, the tough memories might bring up some emotions that are best dealt with support.

The magic happens when we don't try to force ourselves to let painful memories go, but instead we hold it a little softer in our hands, like a beautiful baby bird. A shift occurs bit by bit, and then suddenly, out of nowhere, you can raise your hands, and the beautiful bird takes flight for the first time, allowing you to set it free.

IN THE BEGINNING

> You see it is not about letting go, but rather about softening your grip. For too long, people have said to one another, *"Let it go, for goodness sake!"* Easier said than done, right?

However, I discovered through my own experience – along with the process of helping others – that we've been looking at it through the wrong lens all along.

In the beginning, you might be terrified, and you will very likely be unsure, but remember that when it gets hard, you are getting close to the breakthrough that you are looking for.

I highly recommend that you be brave enough to share your journey with others, as they will help to hold space for you and give you the encouragement and support you will need to continue. In these times for me, my friends were such a blessing and surprised me with their graciousness, fortitude, understanding and deep loving kindness.

So stand strong, dig deep, and remember that this journey does not have to be a solo expedition.

CHAPTER 6

THE PRINCIPLES OF UNBOXING

Life is a journey and it is not a race, the road is long so don't forget to celebrate your success and smell the roses.

Do you feel like you are not at your full potential?

Do you sometimes feel overwhelmed, like you feel heavy or confused, and can not see the road ahead?

Sometimes we even feel like we can barely see the light at the end of the tunnel. What if I told you that the light was real, but the tunnel is not? That it's just the perspective you've elaborately created in your mind because you have zoomed in with eagle-like laser point focus.

You might need to consider zooming out of the tunnel to see the big picture instead. When we become transfixed on something in our life with such laser-like focus, it can feel impossible to look away. Like when we feel angered by someone else's actions or words towards us, we become fixed on the anger and see nothing else around it.

Zooming out is one of the first techniques I teach my clients in mindfulness and it is incredibly powerful to learn – particularly in difficult moments when we are gripped by emotions that feel out of our control.

> Perhaps you also have a full storage facility of your very own in your mind that is holding you back from achieving your infinite potential?

Limitless potential exists in us all; just for many, it is hidden from view. For me, it was completely obscured from my vision, deep in my subconscious below, in my very own Fort Knox. Blocked by boxes, walls, barbed wire, and an elaborate alarm system. If I can find mine in amongst all that so can you.

I found it, just like you can find yours. Wherever it is, it wants to be found and you are getting signposted to discover it all the time.

Fear is the most common thing that holds us back from uncovering our infinite potential.

You are never alone.

You are not alone. You are never alone. There is a beautiful version of yourself buried inside your boxes. It is your inner child filled with unconditional love and joy. When you find them, as I did, you will realise that there is a force deep within yearning to be released. This box will bring such magic back into your life. Your inner child is divine and innocent, and maybe, like mine, full of beans, playful and curious.

THE PRINCIPLES OF UNBOXING

When you finally open this box, you will most definitely know it. I discovered my inner child was my very own Tigger from *Winnie the Pooh*, and I was most pleased to see her. For some of my friends, not so much. Others were over the moon and continue to be filled, with the joy that my very own Tigger brings on occasions.

My Tigger-like inner child has calmed gradually over the years. I think the initial excitement to get out was just a bit much at first. Now, my inner child is content in a beautiful life filled with wonder and joy and she has softened me, enlightened me and shown me a beautiful way forward into my new life.

In the boxes I've unpacked since discovering my inner child, I have uncovered so many beautiful parts of me that I embrace to this very day. Some parts of me had been dampened by negative experiences in life. There were other parts of me that I had completely forgotten about. Today, I feel whole in all my uniqueness, just as the world intended – never feeling alone, no matter what life brings me.

There are eight key principles that I have created to help you on your way:

1. **Support**
2. **Begin**
3. **Time**
4. **Celebrate**
5. **Kindness**
6. **Depth**
7. **Continuum**
8. **Give**

INFINITE YOU

I have deliberately developed them in this order for your understanding. However, they will in time become independent and overlap one another throughout your journey.

1. Support

Find someone to hold space for you who is prepared to go all the way to bring you forward to the light.

The first step is the most important of all. Find someone you trust. Someone, who will hold space, through your journey as you unpack your boxes. This part is so important, so please do not go it alone. There are nearly eight billion people on the planet, and they are here to help.

I found someone through a chance encounter that was a professional, who could help guide me through the process of unpacking. It requires attention, focus and support, so take your time to find the right person who can help. This person will need to challenge you and hold space for you so that you feel safe and protected in your times of vulnerability.

Whoever the person is for you, you will know when you find them. Just be open to the potential, so you do not miss their timely arrival into your life. Let them guide you forth on a magical journey, supported and nourished.

If it's appropriate for you to seek out professional support, do not be scared to open up to the right person. Equally, do not settle if the space somehow does not feel right. Just remember to know the difference between fear, as opposed to a lack of connection.

THE PRINCIPLES OF UNBOXING

"Step into the arena," as the beautiful Brene Brown once said, and be vulnerable. Therefore, it is important that you feel comfortable to begin your journey whether it's with a psychiatrist, counsellor, coach or a combined effort.

We are all not only here to help you, but we are purposefully driven to do this work in the real world.

Remember, professionals can work together to help you find your path to success. It is your life to decide what support you want, so do not be scared to ask professionals to work together on your behalf. I have done this will clients in my coaching business many times, and it can produce very successful results – especially if you are dealing with long-standing mental and/or physical health conditions. If you cannot find the right combination initially, keep looking until you do. Ask people you trust for referrals because they know you much better than you probably think.

The right person or combination is out there for you. You just need to start looking and be prepared to commit to one another to stay the journey all the way – especially when the going gets tough. Once you build trust and understanding together, you can find the right path forward.

When space is held for you with unconditional love, your heart can blossom like a lotus flower in full bloom. When you heart feels safe, you can feel, rather than mentally try to rationalise everything.

We are in an epidemic of emotional illiteracy, don't let that be where your story ends. The day you seek support to hold space for you is the first day of the beautiful journey of discovering you on the inside. The authentic you, that you were always meant to be, is busting to break out of the shackles of emotional conditioning. This is the first step to answer their call.

I can't overstate how important it is to seek out support on your journey forward. Support that will help you to reflect, create perspective, expand and grow, so that you may transform your life completely.

Just over 15 years ago, I was standing at this same crossroads in my life.

I was scared, I felt alone and completely lost after ending the longest relationship of my life. It was a relationship where I lost myself completely. Not because of anyone else. I simply became the relationship and forgot who I was completely. I tell you this to reassure you that you can find your way back, no matter how far off your path you think you have wandered.

My yogic practices have taught me that every experience you have in life is vital. No matter how big you think the mistake was you made, how great the disappointment was or the mess you got yourself into, it was always the right path for you.

Even if you didn't learn the lesson when it was first brought to you in your life, it will continue to return to you, giving you new opportunities to learn. The trauma, anxiety, sadness, regret and disappointment remains in your memory for you to pickup and allow it to leave at the time when you are ready.

Asking for help is the first step forward in allowing a new beginning to flow into your life – one filled with infinite potential and limitless possibilities.

THE PRINCIPLES OF UNBOXING

2. Begin

Begin unpacking those boxes, one by one.

This step is, by far, considered the hardest. It might take all the courage you can muster simply to begin to unpack your boxes. As humans, we have an uncanny ability to procrastinate to avoid difficult and uncomfortable situations in life. However, procrastination is simply an act of putting them off. They will keep coming back again and again until you find the courage to walk your path, rather than to sit on the sidelines.

> Do you want to sit on the sidelines? Or do you want to live your life to your full potential?

For some of us, we do not have a mid-life crisis problem. We have a storage problem!

At some point, if you choose to continue to sidestep the lessons, you are going to run out of storage space – just like I did. It is just a matter of time and pretty simple mathematics. It's essentially a ticking time bomb! Tick, tick, tick... BOOM!

So, all you need to do is start! Sometimes just making the decision to start can create a sense of relief, and potentially an air of excitement, even if it is a little naive. A leap of faith to venture in a new direction can create a new perspective. The key is to remain open, no matter what comes your way.

Remember, as I said early, it could be hard in the beginning but stick with it, and it will get easier as your breakthrough moments arrive, one after another. Your confidence will rise, and your awareness will also become greater, as you connect deeper and deeper into the infinite you; as you discover your authentic sense of self.

It won't be long before people start to notice that you are doing something different in life. Be the change you want to see. When you change, the people around you change, and the world changes, one ripple at a time.

All you need to do to set off the ripple effect is to start the discovery within yourself.

3. Time

It is not a race, so work through this at your own pace.

Life is not a race to the finish line. It is something to be savoured and enjoyed. So, take all the time you need because it's not a competition, either. You do not need to discover and madly open all your boxes at once. Some things are to be done delicately, with care and consideration. Remember, some boxes are heavy, and some are fragile – so make sure you treat them accordingly.

You do not need to become the 'box hunter'. They will not just appear, as you stomp around the place demanding, *"Come out, come out. I know you are there!"* – or stalk them like a lioness on a night hunt.

They will appear just as they should, and as long as you have an open mind, heart and eyes. You will see them on the path right in front of you, in the moments as you experience life's triggers of past memories.

THE PRINCIPLES OF UNBOXING

Continue to live your life and balance reality with your new journey of discovery. Integrate what you learn and see the connections into other areas of your life as you unpack. You will start to see patterns form and see the repetition of where you repeated the same lessons in your life. Like selecting the wrong kinds of partners, the wrong people to associate with and the wrong jobs.

Don't judge yourself through rumination of your past experiences as you unpack. Reflect with love and gratitude so that you may release the burdens in your heart and move forward in your life feeling lighter, free and open, one step at a time.

Lean into and understand the principals of growth, taking your focus off time, allowing for whatever time is needed. Try to remember to do this without letting the car of procrastination to apply the brakes, driven by the driver named fear.

Fear can make you want to completely stop at literally any time, yet it can also make you want to race forward in an attempt to limit the pain. It is important to remember to allow the feelings to naturally rise – not by force. It's also equally important that when fear sets in with an immediate desire to suddenly run in the exact opposite direction, to stop, wait and find the courage to stand in what is coming up in the box you are unpacking.

I have helped many people unpack difficult boxes, with an instant desire to run when it starts to hurt. Anger, in these circumstances, can rise suddenly as a protective attempt to maintain the status quo. Mindfulness techniques in pausing and breathing can greatly help you to sit in the difficult moments.

INFINITE YOU

Awareness helps you and whoever you seek for support to see these red flags as they arrive. Together, you can work through them, one by one.

In life, remember it often takes years to create difficulty and rushing to reverse it could be both traumatic and not yield long lasting results. In mindfulness, it's the long term practice over time that enables you to develop new neurological pathways in the mind, to develop better habits.

The practice of these techniques is ongoing, not only to unpack your past to unleash your infinite potential, but to allow for you to not return back to default behaviour that caused the problems in the first place.

I remember a movie I watched about a runaway bride who wore sneakers to her wedding. This was so me and it could also be you. I was that person who panicked and ran every time it got hard, so in my past, I never stayed to endure the hard times to discover the beautiful good times that potentially existed beyond. I did this because previously I stayed way too long and got hurt. And so, to avoid hurt, I just left before it got hard.

This principal of not racing is important, because the world often feels like it is on hyperdrive – with everything rushing at us on a constant loop. To stop or slow down is a powerful way to step outside the rat-race and give you time to look within peacefully. Here is where you find your manual, and with help, can find the pages that will create a beautiful way forward for you infinitely.

4. Celebrate

Celebrate your successes along the way.

On the way, celebrate your success with yourself, with others and reward your efforts. You are embarking on something that many have yet to find the courage to do.

Courage should always be recognised and rewarded.

Each day, as you wake up, remember that you are on your way to becoming the best version of yourself so be sure to stop and pat yourself on the back, especially when you have tackled something tough and triumphed.

Today, the aim is to be today's best you and tomorrow the clock re-sets all over again. You are not aiming for an end point, you are aiming to be present. When you learn to embrace celebrating the small momentary successes, you are embracing presence in a delightful way.

The ability to practice moving between small and large successes in life is an incredibly powerful practice to embark on. It creates the ability to recognise perspective. In this way, you can practice perspective in a positive way with success. Then, engaging perspective when times get tough becomes easier because it has already been practiced.

So, the next time you think something is too small to celebrate, think again. Remember you are practicing perspective through observation, so that when things get hard, perspective is your friendly companion keeping you on track. This is the beautiful practice of understanding polarities.

INFINITE YOU

While you'll want to celebrate success, you may also want to reframe how you look at the world.

> What lens do you put on to determine success?

On a hard day, success may be just getting out of bed, or taking some time to simply breath when you are struggling to find a solution to a problem you have at work.

In reflection, what seems like failure could very well be success. When you try a way that ends up being the wrong way, you've learned what doesn't work.

That in itself is success when you put it into perspective.

Share your success with others along the way. Share not only your success when you achieve something great, but also your successful failures, too. Someone is waiting to hear your story to help them on their way.

By sharing in all your successes, including failures, you are inspiring others to take a leap of faith. We often don't take the leap of faith to expand ourselves from fear of failure. When we learn and teach others the successful way to fail, this is the beautiful ripple effect of change the world needs right now.

I found sharing my success and celebrating incredibly beneficial. It gave me the drive and conviction to keep going, especially when times got tough in my life. Life will always have difficult times, but these times are when we grow the most.

THE PRINCIPLES OF UNBOXING

Maybe today you need to simply celebrate the success of making it here to this very moment. Many who have come before you did not, and many more will not make it. Your success, big or small is significant and worthy of your attention.

Teach success, perspective and awareness through leading by example. You never know who is watching you right now, observing you and learning by example. Your ability to share the powerful practice of celebrating success has far reaching impacts. Some of which you will see, however, many you will never see at all, yet they are happening all around you. Influence is a silent partner, touching people everywhere you go – from children to friends and a stranger just observing your actions from afar.

What you celebrate, you resonate into the world.

> Ask yourself what do you want to resonate?

5. Kindness

Be kind to yourself.

Kindness towards yourself is a complete non-negotiable. In yoga, we refer to it as *"Ahimsa"* – loosely translated as *"to do no harm"*. If you have been in a cycle of putting everyone first, leaving your cup empty, it's time to switch up a gear and return to fill up your own cup again. If you are feeling tired and run down, it's because you've probably been putting others first for a very long time.

INFINITE YOU

Through social and cultural conditioning, we have been taught putting yourself first is selfish, and that it's a bad thing.

The conditioning of selfishness being considered a negative quality literally runs generations deep. To put it into context, I was a child of a working class family with baby boomer parents. My parents were born after the war, growing up on rations, living and learning a life of scarcity. This position is relatively common. To be selfish in that era would have been considered appalling. My mother learned from her mother that life's resources are scarce. She had to bathe in the same water once a week with three younger brothers and both her parents. She learned to share by force, and from birth, was taught to put others first always. Her mother worked four jobs and she became the carer of her three younger brothers out of necessity.

My mother, like many mothers, struggled to put herself first for a long time. However, I am grateful that she learned the lesson of self-love and learned to be kind to herself. It was beautiful to watch her flourish swimming in the pool of self-love in her later years of life before she passed away. I like to think I might have actually lead her into the watery pool of self-love myself, after finding my way there some years before. She was a difficult student of self-love but she got there in the end through trust and unconditional love. The effort it took for me to get her there grew me as a human being in delightful ways, of which I will always be grateful to have experienced.

If you're a baby boomer, there is room in your heart for self-love, in fact, your heart is crying out for it. Your body, mind and soul wants to fill up your cup dearly so that you may flourish into the infinite you that you were always meant to be.

THE PRINCIPLES OF UNBOXING

I believe it is possible that self-love is a lesson that most people of my mother's era needed to learn. We needed to break the cycle so that we could evolve and expand love out into the world from within us all. Not the love of external things, but the love the resides deep inside us all.

Future generations are relying on us all to do the work to bring more love into the world. This loving energy begins with you filling your cup first, so that you can fill the cup of others and lead by example teaching others to fill their own cups, too.

When progressing through what is stored in your boxes of life's experiences, remember to take the time to recover and re-calibrate when things go awry because just like life, not everything goes according to your grand plan. Sometimes, it is important to let the dust settle, especially when you have dealt with a box that contained something particularly difficult or confronting.

It is a chance to regroup, clear your mind, steady your heart, and get ready for the next leg of your beautiful journey called life.

Take time out and take time off. Downtime is important and sometimes, putting a box down and walking away to come back another day is the best option. Treating yourself gently as you go, and keeping your cup full will make the journey, not only more palatable, but also potentially enjoyable.

Coming from a place of kindness, guided by self love will lead you along a beautiful path, one delightful step at a time.

Remember the boxes are not going anywhere, so if you need to sit one down again for a bit, cut yourself some slack and wrap yourself up in a blanket of self-love. Practicing Ahimsa towards oneself is a great gift you can give yourself, with the results being amplification of that love from within. When you amplify your love of self, your cup becomes full, making it easier and much more enjoyable to pour the overflow to fill the cups of others.

6. Depth

Be prepared to go deep.

You will discover the best results if you are prepared to go deep, be honest with yourself and always remain the adventurer in your life as you go. The depth lies on the inside, not in the hands of others. When you adventure to the depths of what makes you you, you get to discover some of the most beautiful things. Things that have been dormant often for years, hidden away from view.

Your purpose, superpowers and love could be hidden in the depths of you, overlaid with pain, suffering, hurt, disappointment and regret. Don't be scared to go there because when you discover the things hidden from view beneath your suffering, you will come alive in ways you never imagined.

The best simple way I know to explain the concept of going deep comes from my corporate experience in life through project management. It's a kind of dry way to express the concept of depth but for the rational thinkers of the world, it can bring a simplistic kind of clarity to life.

So, there is a methodology in project management called LEAN. One of the concepts this methodology looks at is to go beyond the surface and do an in-depth analysis of a process, system or function. This is called a root cause analysis. When you do this in

THE PRINCIPLES OF UNBOXING

business, you are able to get to the root cause of the problem, rather that just seeing the symptoms that are closer to the surface.

When you focus on the symptoms, all you do is apply bandaid solutions. When you get to the root cause of the problem, you are able to fix the problem at the source. This process in business is well-known and accepted in project management. However, for some reason we don't apply it to ourselves.

In life, we spend a lot of time and money applying bandaids but rarely go deep enough to get to the root cause of the problem. When you learn to do this by going deep, you get to go to where the magic lies below the surface.

Here is where you discover the infinite potential that exists within us all.

In the process of life, you'll certainly collect more boxes along the way. Look for the signs and try to spot a boxing incident as it arises. If you can do this, you will avoid the need for the root cause analysis, because you will be facing the problem before it sinks to the bottom of the pond.

It is a beautiful thing when you learn to become present and face life's challenges as they arrive. You will be proud when this happens for the first time, just like I was. It can be quite a revelation.

> Remember that it is not your experiences that define you, but how you choose to deal with them as they arise. To box or not to box will become your choice. How amazing is that? However, this will only happen, if you are prepared to go deep.

Heading to the depths is definitely a situation where support is essential. If you are tackling something big, it is important to have a support team if necessary. Your loved ones, friends, family, colleagues and professionals can all support this deep work.

The beauty about going deep is that when you get to the root cause of a problem, you can do two very important things. Firstly, rationalise the problem with the fresh perspective of maturity.

Then secondly, you are less likely to repeat the behaviours because you now understand where it came from, and can do the work to change the way you respond in the future.

Held at the depths is the beautiful ability to learn to be fully present, finding the best way forward by reflecting on the past and prepare for whatever the future may hold.

7. Continuum

There is no end.

As you continue on your journey of life, the unpacking does not end. There will be some boxes hidden away from view, just as I discovered and continue to discover, on the forward journey. Don't let this put you off.

The contents of the boxes obscured from your current view, will appear to you exactly when you are ready to unpack them. Don't worry about looking for them all, like a lioness on an evening hunt. It is not necessary. As you progress, box by box, you become more and more aware, learning and growing with each one you unpack. Sometimes

THE PRINCIPLES OF UNBOXING

boxes are obscured because there is one that needs to be unpacked first before the next comes into view. The complexities and intricacies of a complex subconscious mind are nothing short of miraculous.

Imagine a giant *Tetris* game. You clear a row and the new row shows up. Focus on what is in front of you to unpack, this is being present. Sometimes, what is there will seem overwhelming, yet over time, the overwhelm will gradually subside as you build both confidence, and courage to go deeper to the next layer.

Once you have found yourself here, you have officially discovered the art of unboxed living.

> How good is it to live out in the open, unboxed and untamed?

You are wild and free, ready to take on the world. You now know what needs to be done, and when the future arrives with new boxes, you will be ready; armed with a bunch of beautiful skills, courage and a growing heart space of love to keep on digging deeper and deeper.

The choice is yours how deep you go. It is your life to decide the journey you take. However, now you know that your infinite potential lies at the depths of you. Take as long or a little time as you like. Go as deep or shallow as you like. The rewards await you.

Growth can be slow and progressive, fast and furious, or even a combination of both. You are in the driver's seat now fuelled with some newfound skills, knowledge of potential and opportunity to take the car wherever you want to go.

> All you need to decide right now is in which direction are you headed?

Then, simply head in that direction. Your direction and motivation will change, as all things do. Just remember to keep moving forward no matter what happens, because life is motion and only forward motion will lead you to the next box to unpack.

The choice is always yours.

You may decide to, metaphorically speaking, put a box out with the trash, in an effort to avoid opening it. Don't be hard on yourself and don't worry, the contents of that box will simply keep coming back until you open it and face whatever is held within.

You may potentially see each box time and time again, in fact, just as you are reading this, you may be realising that there are some boxes you are aware of that you have already seen many times in your past. You and only you can decide to open them when it shows up. The choice always remains yours, growth and infinite potential or stagnation.

You are the only one in charge.

8. Give

Pay it forward.

This is the most important of all principles. It is the eighth principle because it is represented by a figure-eight which is infinite.

THE PRINCIPLES OF UNBOXING

Once you have begun your journey, people will notice the changes occurring in you. Share your experiences with others right from the very beginning. Those experiences shared will not only help you to grow, they will also help those to grow around you.

There is never a time when it isn't right to share the full story with others. Share your story in every part of your life. Be visible and be heard because it is time to show others how to find their way forward. Just as you deserve to have a life unboxed out in the open, so does everyone else.

Share with friends, loved ones and work colleagues. Infinite human potential is meant for us all. It is not a secret. It is an internal wisdom that exists dormant within us all.

So when I say, *"Pay it forward,"* I mean with all of your heart, and together, we will change the world one person and one box at a time.

> Imagine what the world could look like!

You have the power to make it happen. Share your book, buy one for someone else as a gift or recommend it to others. The more who unlock the wisdom held within them, the more we all benefit from living in a beautiful world where, ordinary people find their ability to become extraordinary.

CHAPTER 7

GET UNPACKING

*The hardest decision is to begin,
it requires the courage to be vulnerable.*

You have the principles, and you are ready to start. So, what is holding you back? Is it the fear of failure? Or the fear of success?

You see research tells us that it is not just the fear of failure that holds us back, but more often, it's the fear of success. Because when you fail, you think nobody cares about you. However, when you succeed, you could be suddenly, catapulted into fame, and with that comes responsibility. They don't call it the limelight for no reason at all.

Just as I have found, there will be supporters, and there will be knockers. If you discover you feel this way, guess what? You have found another box. The box of judgement and it's an interesting one to unpack, which may keep you busy for a while.

INFINITE YOU

You see, the fear of success runs deep, and it is not something that we actively think about because society has trained us to focus our attention on the fear of failure, through generations of social and cultural conditioning. The actual fear of success for most of us stays hidden in the dark, in one of those boxes, with many of us simply too scared to open it.

> Think about it. What would happen if you gained all the success you could imagine for yourself? What would your life look like in one year? Five years? And 10 years? Would this success bring not only good attention but also unwanted attention? What would other people think of you? You may not be thinking that these questions run through your mind, but if you sit down today and ask yourself these questions, what will you feel? Will you be saying the same things to yourself that I did?

"There's no way I ever want to be famous," is something I had told not only myself but anyone who asked. I was adamant that fame and I could never be intimate friends. In the process of unboxing my life, I asked many people how they felt about fame. It was interesting to discover that people frequently admired it in others, but rarely wanted it for themselves.

Exchange the word famous for successful, and it's a completely different ball game. Success is an interesting concept, of which the response seems to vary from person to person.

I once thought success meant fame and fame meant success. I soon realised that success comes in many forms and doesn't always equate to fame.

GET UNPACKING

> What does success look like to you today? What about tomorrow? What about in five or ten years?

Opening that box containing fear of success has the potential to be a complete game changer in your life.

> Imagine what your life would look like if you embraced success everywhere it showed up in your life!

Flip the lid and tuck into that box, because there is actually no difference between success and failure, except the lens that the generations of ancestral, social and cultural conditioning has applied to your senses and your mindset. You might want to read that sentence again, because it's a big one to digest.

Boxing is a unique experience, and therefore, so is the process of unpacking. Think of it like moving house. Some people pack for months before neatly and tidily, then some chuck everything in a bunch of boxes last minute. Some people unpack bit by bit, with great thought and consideration, while others take the kids approach and tip the box un-side down on the floor. Don't be too committed to any specific approach when it comes to unpacking your stuff. Try to let your instincts for flow guide you at the time. Just being in the moment with each box you open.

A beautiful friend of mine likened his one box as a heavy weight that he skull dragged behind him.

Filling it up his entire life, until one day when it became just too heavy to drag. When your life feels heavy, look behind you for that heavy box, because it might closer than you think.

Others have told me they feel very protective about some of their boxes and want to keep the contents inside. Clearly, they don't yet have a weight or storage issue but rest assured, it's coming, and it will hit you when you least expect it. I promise it is just a matter of time before the pile of boxes comes tumbling down or that pandoras box bursts open.

Yes, some have even described theirs as a *Pandora's Box*, that could literally open of its own free will at anytime. It is understandable that this kind of box left unattended too could cause great anxiety. The beautiful thing is that with the right support, even Pandora's Box can be successfully opened and the contents dealt with. It might surprise you that it isn't what is in the box so much that turns out to be scary. It is so often just the wrapping you have put around it.

This is the story that you have told yourself about the experiences you packed away in your subconscious.

Just remember to consider that you might have changed your storage system midstream, and therefore, you could appear to have your entire life stuffed in one box. Whilst having a number of individual boxes, still hidden from view at the same time. These additional boxes will appear, exactly when they are supposed to. The key is awareness of their arrival and the courage to open them.

You could also have a huge box that you open only to find it is filled with lots of smaller boxes within. Our subconscious storage systems vary hugely in size, weight, order and complexity. If your life feels cluttered, it is likely that your subconscious mind is cluttered as well.

GET UNPACKING

If your life is highly orderly and organised, equally your subconscious mind will likely be the same. Then equally if your life feels scattered, then it is highly probable that your subconscious mind may be scattered by design. Our inner world is constantly trying to reflect to us in the outer world so we can see ourselves for who we truly are.

The most important thing is to feel into where you are at, and try to not get caught up overthinking the whole thing. Overthinking is often what gets us in trouble in the first place.

You have got this no matter what happens, however long it takes, and how you feel. One box or one hundred boxes, you can succeed I promise. I am here with you all the way. You've got this!

CHAPTER 8

THE SIGNIFICANCE OF DREAMS

Your mind is the same in the dream state as it is in the awake state.

I bet, at this point you're thinking this is way too much to take in. It is simply too crazy to start analysing my dreams. If it was good enough for Freud. I promise, stick with me. It is, therefore, good enough for you too.

Analysing dreams is something that has indeed been done, in the world of psychotherapy, for many years. So rest assured there is science in doing this.

In recent years I read a study by scientists from the University of Rome in Italy, that was published in the Journal of Neuroscience. It provides compelling insights into the mechanism that underlie dreaming and the strong relationship our dreams have with our memories.

I read some interesting information where the researchers observed that the frontal theta activity in the frontal cortex of the brain looked just like the successful encoding and retrieval of autobiographical memories seen while we are awake. Therefore, these findings suggest that the neurophysiological mechanisms that we employ while dreaming and recalling dreams are the same as when we construct and retrieve memories while we are awake. This is a big deal. To comprehend that the mind works the same in both dream and awake states is quite something to wrap your head around.

Try recording your dreams by writing them down, and analyse away if this insight has piqued your interest. However, there is a particular topic of dreaming that I would like to draw your attention to which might surprise you.

Have you ever dreamed about houses?

Houses, you say? Yes, houses. By all means, don't take my word for it. Go ahead and do some research on house dreams. However, I can tell you they are quite fascinating when you start to take a look.

I don't mean dreaming of winning an actual house, either. I mean dreaming of yourself living in a house, which sometimes could be under renovation, and could even be dilapidated, or maybe in the dream, you are scared to enter a specific room. You may even find that in your dream, something happens to you in a specific room, in the house you are dreaming about at the time.

I think it is a good idea to start at the beginning. In basic terms, a house in a dream is a representation of you. Pretty cool, hey! I am guessing though that this is probably not what you imagined.

THE SIGNIFICANCE OF DREAMS

Consider that each room represents a different part of you. The lowest floor in your house represents your subconscious, and the highest room, in the house, represents your highest level of consciousness. The detail of the front of your house, in your dreams then represents the way you show yourself to the world. Your back garden in your dreams is where you invite those in and share yourself fully.

The size of the house can relate to your complexity. The state of your house – for instance, if it is run down – can relate to your state of being. If your house has no windows, it can mean that you are hiding your true self from the world. On the other hand, if you have windows, you are sharing your true authentic self.

At one point, I had three layers of curtains on my windows in my bedroom, which was the highest room in my house dreams. Curtains can mean hiding from the world. It was true I was hiding my highest level of consciousness.

On my journey, however, I eventually removed all the curtains to clear glass walls on all four sides, floor to ceiling. I became transparent with others about my highest level of consciousness. Deciphering dreams can be powerful and equally fun in the unpacking process.

Well, don't think house dreams are all doom and gloom though, because as you begin to unpack your boxes, your house dreams may change a lot.

House dreams may also help you to understand the extent of your boxes. For instance, I had an extremely large house, with a basement that seemed to go many floors below the ground. It was big, elaborate and complex, with every kind of science fiction security you can imagine. I had the lot, so clearly I was intending for that stuff to stay put for a very long time until I ran out of storage.

In my journey of unpacking my boxes, I initially discovered the house dream concept from a beautiful friend. She kindly explained that she indeed had her very own volcano in her basement on one side and a lot of boxes on the other. For many years of her house dreams, she was terrified to even open the door to her basement. Once she eventually opened the door, went down a few steps, then ran back to the top and locked it again. It wasn't until later that she alluded me to her volcano story.

At the time, I thought it would have helped if I'd known about this when I discovered my own Fort Knox. It always helps when you know someone else is dealing with something big in their theoretical basement like you. You know, the problem shared is a problem halved concept. It's nice to know you are not alone.

I will be forever grateful to my beautiful friend who shared her house dreaming stories with me as it helped me to understand and interpret mine. Our exchange went on for many years. It was a fun and equally exciting thing to share and assisted us both to truly understand what was going on in both our lives.

So, if you are saying well this all sounds good and interesting, however, I can not remember my dreams. I will share a little trick with you. You are more likely to remember your dreams immediately when you wake up, so start a dream journal and make notes immediately when you wake up. The more you do it, the better you get at it.

When I was actively unpacking, I could see my boxes disappearing in my house dreams. One dream in particular – when I was well

THE SIGNIFICANCE OF DREAMS

into my 427 days of unpacking – I noticed my basement was almost empty, and construction work was happening. You see, I was unpacking my boxes, and they were disappearing right before my eyes in my dreams. I was renovating my subconscious, and like magic, the basement was no longer deep underground, but it was now just the ground floor in my house.

Further along in my dreams, I had discovered, while dreaming, that I had relocated my bedroom from the top floor of my house to the basement. You see I was doing some work on resetting my editor, deep in my subconscious mind, so it was time to move in and get to the heart of it for me.

See this is the beauty of unboxing your life you can reset your mind and create an entirely new story for yourself, one dream, one box, one day at a time.

My advice to you is to find a dream buddy and share your house dreams because they might prove to be more helpful than you may at first think. To be open to understanding the power of dreams may take some time. You are not going to simply tell yourself before you sleep one night that today I will remember all of my dreams. Equally, you won't just decide to start dreaming about houses.

Start your dream journal and unpack the boxes that come up, then see what happens as you go. Life is a journey not a destination. Enjoy your dreams and the reflections they may be providing to bring you understanding within your life.

There are many books, apps and information online about dreaming, along with professionals who can help you tap into what your dreams are telling you. We know the mind is powerful.

INFINITE YOU

Beginning to understand the subconscious mind could lead you to your untapped infinite potential in life, ever so beautifully hidden within you, just like your user manual.

> If you only had known it was there all along, where would you life be right now?

> You are exactly where you should be right now!

Don't worry about the past, the present moment is where you begin to create the future you desire. Expand your awareness to both the awakened and dream state and you grow your opportunity to discover untapped potential held within.

Get excited, get dreaming and watch the world within unfold before your very own eyes.

Forget about the monster under your bed. When you start to tap into dreams, you might find yourself wanting to sleep a whole lot more.

Dream and adventure into the unknown and share your experiences. You too might help someone else, just like I have been able to, since I discovered the power of dreams.

CHAPTER 9

THE WORLD OF BOXES

*Understanding how to recognise types of boxes
will make the unpacking easier.*

It is valuable to understand that a box is not just a box. The boxes, you will need to unpack in your subconscious are not so dissimilar to removal boxes. Some contain breakables, which potentially hold painful memories from your past. You most likely will know the ones that I am talking about here. They are the ones with the word *'Fragile'*, written on the side.

Then, some are particularly heavy and have the word *'Heavy'*, written on the side of the box. These should always be carried by two people because a problem shared is often a problem halved. The heavy boxes are the ones that feel like they are quite literally, weighing you down in life, hence the heaviness.

Then there are tiny wee little boxes that contain those beautiful and special memories which we cling to, that are attached to specific times in our life. These can be things that are precious to us like jewellery boxes or those old shoe boxes filled with keepsakes, just like old love letters.

Remember I am talking metaphorically, to help you understand that unpacking what is holding you back in life in your subconscious is not so dissimilar to unpacking moving boxes. To successfully be able to move forward in life, unpacking what is weighing you down is incredibly powerful.

Some boxes big or small will feel heavy in your heart, so much so that just the idea of picking them up fills you with a sense of panic and deep despair. Be careful with these boxes. In fact, be careful with all of your boxes and the order in which you choose to unpack them.

Some days, you will feel like you can take on the world. On these days, you might be filled with a wonderful sense of enthusiasm and drive. However, occasionally there will be days when you will possibly feel the exact opposite. On these days, your heart could feel like it could, quite easily, be crushed by the tiniest of pressure. Be gentle and kind to yourself on these days.

Remember it is not a race to a finish line; life is motion, so that doesn't always mean a sprint.

If today is just not a good day to lift the tape on the box that makes your heart feel heavy, then put it aside. However, you can always peel back the tape holding it shut, and take a little peek. You will know when you are ready to tackle each box. Sometimes you will be surprised once you take a deep breathe and feel into what is in the box that has shown up in your life. You might feel more courageous and stronger than you first thought.

THE WORLD OF BOXES

Either way, remember there is greatness waiting for you on the other side of each box.

You will expand and transform a little further, with every box you open and reclaim what you lost in its contents. I liken this to floating down the river of life. Sometimes, you get snagged on a tree on the bank of the river, leaving behind a piece of you. Opening the box and reclaiming that piece of you that is held within it, can give you the sense of feeling a little more whole than before. Piece by piece and box by box, you get to rebuild the person you were always meant to be.

Always remember that there is no need to unpack your boxes alone. This is a really important bit of advice that I cannot overstate. If you heed this advice well, you will go far.

In my past, I was known for my stubbornness, something I spent a lot of time in reflection to unpack, understand and overcome. Be brave and do not let your propensity for stubbornness get in your way of finding your superpowers and living life out in the open, whole and authentically you.

As my dear friend said on my very own journey and as will your supporters, *"Stick with it, you've got this."*

There is nothing weak about reaching out for help. It is extremely brave indeed, not to mention an intelligent thing to do.

> Think about it. When you feel overwhelmed, remember the nearly eight billion people on this one planet. Surely, we are here for more than just to compete with each other, wouldn't you agree?

INFINITE YOU

Life gets tricky for everyone at some point in time. Today it might be you, and tomorrow, it might be someone else. In life, there are different roles for us all to play, and it is vital to understand that they are fluid day by day. My mum and I used to call it 'swings and roundabouts'. Sometimes you are the helper, and sometimes you need help, yet both roles are equally important.

I once read about a beautiful Icelandic word for intuition known as *"Innsaei"*. I was captivated by its meaning and a movie that I watched about it. Innsaei means *"to see within"*, to have a strong inner compass to navigate your way in an ever-changing world.

When you get the opportunity to feel as though you can see the perspective in another person's shoes, it can be quite powerful indeed. This concept helped me to open my eyes to both sides of the story, to understand that sometimes it is vital to provide help to others and sometimes it is also equally important to ask for help.

One day I sat and wrote this poem which I think articulated it well for me and it might shed some light on the role that *Innsaei* may play in your life, too:

THE WORLD OF BOXES

Innsaei

Yesterday I was the student
Tomorrow I'm the teacher

One day I'm the postulant
Another I'm the preacher

One moment I'm listening
Just as in another I'm the speaker

Life is full of moments
And full of roles

As we learn to trust our instincts
We can understand where one needs to end
And another begin

In life's cycles we are all
Not merely one
But rather the sum

Let someone kind support you and hold space in your time of need. One day you, in turn, will get the opportunity to do it for someone else. Maybe in your life, it will be like mine, and it will happen time and time again, as you grow and step forward each day.

The value others have brought to my life is astounding. Every day I grow through engagement, support, conversation and understanding, from others. Children, adults, supporters and adversaries all help us to grow – exactly as we need to – to live a life of purpose, fully and authentically our own.

There is much to learn and much to teach. We are meant to do both, and there is no requirement for you to achieve a certain amount before you begin. Each day, you gain knowledge, understanding and wisdom that you can share. Share this freely for someone in your life likely has a box they have no idea how to open and your wisdom, love and understanding might very well be the key they are waiting for.

We are human, first and foremost.

Yes, we are lots of other things overlaid on top of that, however, this journey will help you to realise that at the core, we are much more the same than we are different.

There will be boxes you discover that you might be embarrassed to share the contents within. We all have them – these are the boxes of regret and shame. By opening and understanding their contents, you can and will be able to let the regrets of your life leave your subconscious. Whatever they are for you, remember many have had the same regrets in life.

Once in your past without the tethering holding you back, you will be able to move forward without judgement of yourself – regardless of your past actions. You are enough, you were always enough and no mistake made in your past defines who you are today.

The opening and release of these types of boxes may be hard, but the rewards will be greater than you could ever imagine possible. When you get the opportunity to evaluate a situation from your past, with your current rational ability, you will realise that they

THE WORLD OF BOXES

are not anywhere near as big as they felt in the past, or as bad as the story you wove around the experience. Reflection and perspective are beautiful skills to adapt when delving deep into the boxes of shame and regret. The longer these types of boxes remain unopened, the greater our capacity to weave a big story in our mind about the contents held within.

I myself discovered that often the story that I wove around the box, carried far more weight than the actual contents held within the box. You too will realise this yourself when you get to a box that feels heavy on the outside, yet when you open the lid, you'll say to yourself, *"Is that it?"* – usually followed by a good chuckle.

Remember to laugh to lighten the moments. Laughter helped me immensely.

The more you progress on your journey living this amazing thing we call life, the more boxes you'll get to open and the more you will begin to recognise your are on your path. You will begin to not fear their arrival, yet actually revel in their appearance, and greet them saying,

> *"Well, hello there box. Let's see what mysteries you have inside for me today!"*

CHAPTER 10

THE DEATH BOXES

From the moment we are born we are are dying, yet death seems to surprise us all.

We all have them, the boxes where we store our deepest of suffering. These feelings are often coupled, with a deep sense of longing and attachment to our loved ones, that have left us behind, to travel forward on their journey. These things are all contained in our death boxes. They are frequently laced with a kind of heaviness. Stored within your heart or far away on the lowest floor of your storage system, deep within your subconscious. It all depends on your process of dealing with death where you choose to store your death boxes.

When confronted by death, some are completely overwhelmed with a deep sense of despair within their heart and are never able to release it on their own. Alternatively, some choose to hold it as far away a possible from their heart, in storage, deep within their subconscious. Sometimes, this is through an elaborate avoidance mechanism because it can feel impossible to deal with the loss of someone you loved dearly, at the time. Both of these scenarios can be incredibly debilitating in life, for neither give us a sense of closure.

When we hold the despair within our heart, it is as though we just cannot let go and move forward in life. Our heart feels heavy with loss. Often, we feel like letting go is forgetting them and this can trigger significant volumes of guilt.

When we choose to hold our pain of loss away from our hearts completely, we can remain for years in a complete state of denial. This can leave us completely unable to talk about the loved one lost at all. We forever feel the gap in our hearts at a distance. It is like the loving memories no matter how far we think we have removed them from our hearts remain energetically tethered to us. I see this often, particularly in men, due to their apparent need to be the strong one who has to hold everyone together.

Often the way we deal with death is deeply related to our social and cultural conditioning. It can be formed, by our learned religious beliefs, parental role models and our exposure directly to death itself. Our understanding of what death means to us is very personal and important to discover. Imprints occur as a direct result of our experience in life, so a death experience not supported well as a child can leave a long-lasting impression. These experiences are unique, and therefore, our perception of death can also similarly have a varying and unique impact on us.

Consider an example of a child growing up in a war-torn country with death all around them all their life, as opposed to the experience of a child growing up in a western country, being sheltered from death – like it is something to be avoided. Our lives are frequently lived, in vastly different contrasts, and our experiences and beliefs can both instil fear and a sense of calm. It is all about the environment

THE DEATH BOXES

in which we live, particularly during our impressionable years of childhood.

Most people see death as an ending, one to make you feel like everything that meant anything to you, left your body at that exact moment a loved one died. As though part of you, it would seem, had also died. In life, we know that death is inevitable, and it comes to us all at some point. Sometimes, death comes when we are young, some without notice and some through what can be a long and painful amount of suffering.

Ok so let me put it out there. I do not presently, and have never seen the concept of death, the way most people I meet do. For my entire life, this has puzzled others around me. I have experienced death in family members, friends and have never been overwhelmed by their passings. As a young adult, I was intrigued why this was the case for me and not for others. Many people thought I was cold or in denial or both. However, I can articulate now as an adult, that I have a sense of deep understanding of the process of death which brings me peace around the lead up to, the passing and beyond.

Basically, from the moment, we are born, we are dying. Our body experiences a slow demise until, eventually, it stops working entirely and we die. We know this happens for a multitude of reasons.

Death is both an ending and a beginning for me for several reasons.

There are many explanations available to read to understand the process of death, which are both scientifically and energetically positioned. I have read many of them, and gained much wisdom. I have personally experienced that embracing the immanence of death through yogic philosophical practices can improve the quality of your life significantly. The fact that this occurred for me even though I grew up in a western culture – where discussing death was for the most part considered taboo – is surprising to many. My experience may shed some light on the potential for understanding to be achieved, in any circumstances.

First, we should take a step back because death is not just about the end of life, even though that is what we focus on when we consider death. Death is, in simple terms, just an ending. Friendships die, relationships die, enthusiasm for a job you no longer enjoy dies and sometimes, our entire zest for life, can die as well. These experiences do not necessarily mean that we die, too.

> Have any of these things happened to you?

In my lifetime, I have seen it unfold in many ways. The way people deal with death has always intrigued me. I know it might seem odd that I am somewhat intrigued by how people deal with death, but when you think about it, it is kind of strange!

> Death is something that we clearly know is coming, right?

Although we live life like it is never going to arrive and when it does, we are surprised. Yet the strangest thing of all is that we do not see it coming, because we choose not to live in present moment awareness. We are way too busy reminiscing about what happened in the past and dreaming of the future.

THE DEATH BOXES

> So, why are we so surprised and scared of death?

Yet when we are confronted by it, we suddenly want to live for every moment we have like it is our last. It is like we suddenly realised we were going to die, yet we knew it all along.

The concept of facing the reality of death is something that I have never felt about the way most have around me. You see most people I have met do not want to talk about death. In the dictionary, death is the end of life and morbidity is the suffering in the potential lead up to the end of life, so it is kind of hard to talk about death without being morbid, right? There is a big difference in understanding, that any day, you could die, as opposed to considering death right now.

In some cultures, death is considered honourable, and in others, it is the path to something greater. But in western culture, it is for most people I have met, the absolute end.

Depending on what you believe in spiritually or religiously, death can mean many things. People I know who are not at all religious or spiritual often say things like, *"Well, hopefully they are in a better place now,"* always seems so odd to me. This sudden about-turn invariably confuses me completely.

> Where does the better place suddenly appear from when someone who is neither spiritual or religious loses someone they love? Is it a subconscious knowing that rises to the surface, or is it clinging to hope to lighten the load of the loss of a loved one?

INFINITE YOU

> Do we, in the end, hope that there is something else or do we innately know that it exists and when our mortality is shown to us front and centre we start to see?

I have felt the pain of death close to me many times in my life. I feel into life, as though death could come at any time. I lost both my parents and all my grandparents before the age of 50. Death is familiar for me, but even when it is not, it does not have to be as scary or overwhelming as we might think. In fact, I have been there for some of the closest people to me in their final days. I feel a sense of calm in these situations which surprises people.

I also have had many conversations with people who knew they were either going to die, or could possibly die, and I am always happy to talk about what death means to them. This kind of openness can be both helpful and comforting to those who are dying of slow and often debilitating disease in their body. I never shy away from these potentially difficult conversations. To feel comfortable with death and support others facing death or overcoming the impact of death is incredibly rewarding.

Don't get me wrong, I have on at least one occasion in my life thought not waking up the next day would surely be easier. When at 26, I separated from my husband, after only seven years of marriage I felt completely overwhelmed by the death of my marriage.

> Have we not, all at some time, felt completely overwhelmed by life?

THE DEATH BOXES

I learned a lot in these moments about myself, which helped me grow into the person I am today. I also learned, in these moments, a little about how the feelings of overwhelm can lead to suicidal thoughts. Even though I did not consider suicide myself, I felt the lowest I had ever felt in my life, and I am an optimistic person by nature.

I have asked many people about how they feel about their impending death, and I have to say I usually get a standard response. Some people even get angry with me and are paralysed by the idea of even discussing it. They do not seem to realise it is coming for us all minute by minute, hour by hour and day by day. Yet we wish the working week over, we breathe short, shallow breaths and we put off improving our health until tomorrow as if it ain't coming at all.

There was lots of death in my Fort Knox of boxes, and there might very well be with you, too. However, the ones that surprised me the most are the boxes that contained the endings, that I could not let go of in life. I had previously learned to see the endings in my life as total failures, not valuable lessons.

The death of my marriage at 26-years-old was, in my eyes, a complete failure on my part. So I did what I did well, and I boxed it up and put it far away, so I did not have to deal with it at all. In doing this, I somehow lost many years of my life entirely. I forgot about not only the suffering of divorce but also all the amazing things I had done in my life in those seven years. It was as if, I had completely wiped it from my memory; as if it had never existed at all.

> That is some coping mechanism, don't you think?

> Has this happened to you? Did you think you got divorced because your parents did? What did you learn from growing up with parents separating and divorcing? Did you learn lessons on how to be a better person and care for others better? Or did you not share yourself, because you felt like others simply could not be trusted?

> Endings can be incredibly hard but so can beginnings, too, right?

When we are born, it's possibly the hardest beginning of all. Probably a good reason why we don't remember it, leaving it hidden deep within our subconscious.

> What is the difference between beginnings and endings? Or are they the same?

Is it just the lenses we look through that makes them different? One person's ending is another person's beginning. Sounds odd doesn't it but it is true. You end a relationship, and they begin one with someone else. It is your ending but also their beginning.

As you face your endings in life, face them with a view that a new beginning is coming. If you don't want to consider your death, then at least focus completely on living this very minute and every other minute you are experiencing, because you never know when it may very well be your last.

THE DEATH BOXES

Be gentle with your death boxes, be kind to yourself and be gracious with the lessons held within as you open each one of them.

You, as I did, might be pleasantly surprised as to some lessons you learn from the endings you both choose and of those that are chosen for you. The endings we don't choose – like relationships ending because our partner has left us – can be difficult to confront and they are frequently these things we find in our boxes that we simply haven't let go of in our life.

Alternatively, you could do absolutely nothing! Hold on to all the things holding you back in life and keep living as if life will never end, but as John Joseph Adams once said, *"The end is nigh."*

During the writing of this book, the person closest to me died, my dearest mother. I had the good fortune of having an amazing mother who was incredibly proud of everything I did and loved me very much. In fact, she was loved and revered by most people she met in life, including me.

At the end of her life, we reached a special point in our relationship, one of acceptance and understanding. It is only in the days and the weeks beyond her loss in my life am I recounting the amazing and incredibly valuable lessons my mother taught me. You see everyone teaches you something.

My mother taught me tolerance because her stubbornness drove me completely mad at times. But her resilience to a continual barrage of on-going illnesses was nothing short of impressive. From the beginning, when she got breast cancer before the age of 60, she simply dug in her heels and with steely determination marched forward in life.

INFINITE YOU

She was my role model in life.

I learned a never give up attitude directly from my mother and a determination that has since driven many people beyond annoyed in my life.

I had the most honourable job of supporting my mother in her final eight years of life. They were some of the greatest years of my life to date. We laughed, we cried and we both grew as human beings in so many magical ways. You see my mother taught me many things, but I had a trick or two up my sleeve that she didn't see coming.

I was on a personal journey of self-discovery and spiritual enlightenment and my mother was the greatest sounding board whom, at that point, I had ever known. She listened, learned and grew with me. Yes, I even managed to take not only the edge of, but lead her in a new direction of spirituality. This was no small feat considering my mother was a raging atheist for my entire life, and it is only through perseverance and knowledge that I helped her to see the light – excuse the pun.

Through good science and openness, my mother gained insight and wandered into the middle with me, rather than taking a strong view on the edge. I honestly believe this gave her an incredible sense of peace in the lead up to her passing that she did not have prior.

It is a beautiful thing when you can help bring peace at the end of someone's life.

In Buddhism, it is suggested to be one of the kindest things you can do to help them transition beyond this life to the next. We wrestled each other with religion, philosophy and spirituality for many years and it brought out the best in us both.

So, here I am confined to my home during a global pandemic, just days after my mum's passing, writing this chapter with a smile on my face and knowledge in my heart that I avoided boxing this experience in my life.

Woohoo, this is big!

I sit with it gently in my heart as each day passes with both sorrow and joy as it interchanges. You would think that it would be too much to bear but miraculously it is not. For now, I understand that her passing is not only an ending but also a beginning for us both.

My mum made a grand exit in life and passed on Mothers Day. She didn't do life by halves and always lived on her own terms. The morning after her passing, I woke up with a strong sense of it was time to move forward. I had unknowingly put my life on hold for many years to take care of my mum.

Now, it's all about me. I had given her the peaceful and quiet passing she wanted and the next chapter of my life has begun.

My advice to you is when you experience death head-on, don't rush to run away, to hide or box it up. For you will have to face it sooner or later. There is a lesson in all of life's experiences.

> What is the lesson for this one?

INFINITE YOU

Remember that with every ending, follows a new beginning. Allow whatever comes up in the death boxes, feel into the emotions, the lessons, and allow yourself to move forward whole, embracing the life you have in each day; moment by moment.

Like it was for me, let death be a teacher of the greatest lessons.

CHAPTER 11

THE NEED FOR HUMOUR

The art of laughing will bring love back into your heart.

I am certainly not the first person to think that life is too short to be serious all the time, right? Don't get me wrong, sometimes it is both valid and necessary on occasions to be serious. But in life, it is equally important to not get completely swept away with all your seriousness. If this happens, life can get the better of you.

Yes, I managed to find myself in this very dilemma. I remember being very funny as a child. I was the class clown and used to make everyone laugh. Then, one day I suddenly realised it had all changed and I just seemed to get serious about everything. I don't think it was just one thing that happened to cause my seriousness. I honestly think it rolled in like a dark cloud, over time, slow and steady, but when it appeared in my line of sight, it was hard to move on.

There are lots of situations in life that can cause this to happen, including trauma, loss or disappointment. I did not think my life had more disappointments than the next kid. However, I was incredibly sensitive as a child. The combination of feelings and seeing the cruelty that existed in the world took its toll on the very essence of me. Which then seemed to disconnect the wiring on my carefree humour switch. At this point, it was at least malfunctioning, seemingly broken.

In fact, I think my humour over time became sarcastic as the anger below the surface festered as a way to deal with the disappointment in my life. I know clearly now that the sarcasm that I was projecting was most definitely pent up anger at the world. The beautiful world I had once lived with endless joy and abandon as a child full of wonder had shown me its cruel side, and all I could do was run away and hide.

> Have you lost your sense of humour? Has your zest for life become sarcasm?

As I found out much later in life, this is an elaborate coping mechanism. I recognise this in a lot of people I meet. As people try to find ways to cope – in a world where it sometimes seems like there is more wrong than right – I recognise this coping mechanism well.

When you open some boxes and release the emotions and suffering you have long stored away in them, it will give you opportunities to see the funny side of life when you least expect it. When this happens, don't be afraid to laugh. Hindsight is a marvellous thing and learning to look at your past through a softer lens can be very helpful indeed.

When you lose your sense of humour to anger, you often feel like you can't find your way back and laughter seems like the furthermost thing from your mind. However, it can be exactly what you need to break the ice on the surface of sarcasm.

THE NEED FOR HUMOUR

Humour can be a lovely and useful tool in some of the most trying circumstances. My past partners have often been quite the comics and managed – on several occasions – to stop me from getting too serious about everything in life. It's nice to have someone in your life who can remind you to lighten up from time to time. Whether they be a kind friend or a partner, try to welcome their intention for they only mean well.

Even though I now have the fortune of a partner who is absolutely hilarious, it has been incredibly beneficial to find this humour within me – instead of relying on others to break a tendency of getting unnecessarily serious.

Do not ever be afraid to be funny, because we all have the beautiful capacity to be funny. For some, it just takes a little more courage to express than others. Some of the simplest kinds of humour are the best in life. You know, the kind of humour that can be corny and a little dad-like. However, as someone once said to me, if you think that you aren't funny, just be fun instead. We can always be fun, even if we think that we are not funny at all.

It is, completely okay to laugh at your own jokes and to make light of your situation using humour. I do this all the time as it can lift your spirits, and those of the people around you, in a lovely way. Sometimes other people laugh, sometimes only I laugh, but in the end, it doesn't matter if others do not get your kind of funny. The right people in your life will laugh with you and occasionally at you, but in the kindest and most loving of ways.

As Buddha has been quoted to have said by many, *"In life, suffering is pretty much a certainty. If you manage to find a way to sit with your suffering, it will become your blessing, and ultimately your teacher."*

So, laughing at life can help you to sit in the fire a little longer to receive your blessings, and the lessons that follow may enhance your life in ways you never imagined possible.

Today, I laugh at the most inappropriate things. So, when my joke doesn't appeal to others, instead, they can delight in my contagious love of life, and my laugh. Often we decide we are not funny, without trying our humour out on others. Give it a go because you might be surprised at the response you receive.

Humour has crept its way back into every corner of my life, and it is a beautiful thing indeed. I find humour in my mistakes to lighten the load, and in the situations when the potential for seriousness is high. I simply, take the edge off with a good belly laugh. It works a treat.

If you are feeling like laughter is missing in your life, welcome it back with an open heart and watch, as you too lighten the load of seriousness in your life. When they say laughter is the best medicine, I completely understand what they mean now. Learning to laugh at yourself, even just a little, brings great dividends in life, softening your sharp edges and creating cracks, making space for joy to flow in again.

Yes, the world can be cruel, but there is also magic to be had, and you might just find it, as I did in humour. It is all around us. What you focus on you feed, so I try to remain focused on growing the magic and reducing the cruelty by not giving it my attention. When I used to focus on the cruelty, I became angry in my heart.

Only light can light up a dark room. Cruelty, with anger fueling the fire, is not helpful at all for yourself or those around you.

THE NEED FOR HUMOUR

Today, my heart is open to receive the energy of love. I radiate this essence, and I walk my path with ease and grace. It has become one of my many mantras in life. Love returning to my heart has enabled me to walk the path, no matter how hard it gets. Humour takes me the rest of the way down the meandering path of life, with a child-like curiosity and enthusiasm for life and all it brings.

Begin by inviting the warmth of humour back into your life; allow the softening to occur and the expansion in your heart. Your friends and loved ones will notice the difference in you and joy will return to your life, just as it was always meant to be.

Laughter is love finding its wings, so release it out into the world everywhere you go.

CHAPTER 12

FIND YOUR TRIBE

Your people are looking for you, open your heart, be vulnerable and they will appear.

I have to say that the *Urban Dictionary's* definition of a tribe hit the spot for me. The number one definition lists tribe as, *"A group of friends that becomes your family."*

> Is there some familiarity there for you? Do you sometimes feel like you have lost your tribe, and you are stuck out in the wilderness all alone, facing the troubles of the world without moral support, unconditional love and laughter?

Well, get out there and find your tribe!

You can't do it sitting on your couch watching the TV, or with your face in social media, and wishing the working week away. There are people out there waiting for you to join their tribe.

> Are you, like I was, closed to the potential of having a tribe? Or even worse, shut away from the world determined that this is just how life is for you?

It's time to open up you heart to the possibility of finding your tribe.

The beautiful thing about tribes is they will kick you in the butt when you talk crap or wallow in your self-pity. Your tribe will always remind you how awesome you are, and hold space for you in their hearts, supporting you in your dark times. It is not necessary that you only have one tribe unless that works best for you. However, you can have as many tribes as you like. I have many interests and therefore I have a number of groups I call my tribes people. What your tribe looks like for you is as unique as you are.

For some of you, some of your tribe might be your family members. However, for others like me, you may find little connection at all to some of your family. You may have lost them or never known them at all. Either way, accept that there is absolutely nothing wrong with you if you are different from your family or don't have one. There are tribes out there just for you. I was very different from my family in many ways. When I was young, this caused me to pretend to be something I wasn't to fit in.

> Have you ever pretended to be something you are not, just to fit in somewhere?

I am here to tell you right here and now that it's time to STOP!

FIND YOUR TRIBE

Your tribe will love, support and honour you unconditionally, and exactly as you are. The good the bad and the ugly, warts and all. That is how it works.

So, if your family don't turn out to be members of your tribe, it's okay to cut yourself some slack. Give yourself some room to breathe and go and find your tribe elsewhere.

If you are displaced or not aligned with your family, there is a reason for it. Those reasons may not be apparent today, but as you unpack your life, you will begin to understand and learn the vital lessons that your family life has taught you. One day, you will make peace with your past, and feel grateful for the value your family life brought you as you progressed through life.

No rule book says you must be related by birth to every member of your tribes.

> Have you ever met someone and felt like you instantly connected? Like you felt as though you had known them your entire life after meeting them for the very first time?

They are your tribal people. Allow them in close and keep in touch. These are the people who will be there for you through your trials and tribulations.

The only way to find your tribe is to get out among it, to live life fully and authentically. Humans are not solitary animals, and we thrive best living in groups. Science and history have proven time and time again that we are more successful together than we are working individually.

INFINITE YOU

Get out and go to that meetup, even if it feels uncomfortable. Go to that work function, even if you do not know anyone there. Keep doing it again and again and again, because your tribes are everywhere. The more you interact and discover the world, the bigger and stronger your tribes become.

Remember, not only will you benefit from finding your tribes, but you may also be just the person they are waiting to meet as well. Your story that you share may seem like nothing at the time. However, could end up being life-saving, and you may never know it.

Never underestimate the power of connection available to you and that you can also bring to others.

I focus on remembering to be open to new tribe members always. It is beneficial to evolve and grow through life. The tribe that you have as a child may not be the right tribe to serve you into adulthood. Be prepared to continue to move forward and find where you belong within each stage of your life.

I tell a funny story at parties about what my funeral might look like. You see, I have lots of different tribes people, and if I died and they all attended my funeral, it would be a diverse mix of people who attend. Think about the people you know in your life.

Are you welcoming in diversity to help you stretch and grow?

There has been many studies over the years that suggests we connect with others because of what we see in them is a reflection of what is in us. Isn't that an interesting observation? Equally, what we dislike in others is often a mirror of the things that we dislike

FIND YOUR TRIBE

in ourselves. The world is a giant mirror reflecting back at you, showing you the path to grow.

The more you take some time to get to know yourself and feel comfortable with your authenticity, the easier it becomes to find your tribe – because the things you like in yourself you will most certainly see and like in others.

> Is it time to find a new hobby or step outside that comfort zone and stop doing things the way you always did?

If you always do what you've always done, you will always have what you always had. So, start a new practice, meet new people and experience life in new ways. Your tribes people could be at that arts course you always wanted to do. They could be at a new sports club you join, a library or even at a local park where you walk your dog, because the universe is trying to make it easy for you by putting them right in front of you.

All you need to do is show up and be open to new tribe members.

In my life, I steadily took steps year by year to extend my tribe. If it feels hard for you to do, take small steps, remembering that steps no matter how small are still forward motion. Take the steps you feel comfortable doing at first, and as you gain more confidence, you can take bigger and bigger steps forward.

It is equally important to understand that there are people who no longer serve you and to keep them in your life could be detrimental. Some will leave of their own accord, but some will need a push. It is not selfish to remove yourself from the lives of those who are wrong for you. It is simply a part of the journey of life. Some friendships are for a moment, some for a while and some for a lifetime. They teach us many things on the way, but holding on to those who no longer help us grow, neither serves you or them.

> Is it time for you to let go?

Think of it as managing your room rather than clearing it out. There is a beautiful booked called *Who's In Your Room*, by Ivan Misner. It works on the premise that everyone who comes into your life is in your room. No one can leave because every person who enters your room comes through a one-way door. I know this concept could seem scary, but it isn't. It is just about managing your room.

Bring those tribe members closer to you that support and help you grow. Then allow those who do not to find their way to the back of your room. Everyone can be in the room. It is just about who you give your attention to within your room. It is your room, and you have all the control to work the crowd anyway you like.

> What have you always wanted to try, but none of your friends were interested? Asking yourself this question may give you valuable insight as to the tribe members missing from your life!

FIND YOUR TRIBE

I have an analogy for **TRIBE**:

Teach
Reach
Intersect
Behold
Endure

Our tribe are all capable of **teaching** us many life lessons. These are lessons you will not learn if you stay put. It's like reading one book over and over again, looking for every answer to every question on one page. We know that we must branch out and gain more knowledge to answer the questions in life that come up.

There is a reason we can't see all the answers in our own user manual. We need to interact with others to help us to find the page in our manual, where the answer lies. Connection is so important in the world, and feeling that deep sense of connection with others, is part of your soul's journey home.

In moments of pure magic, many are capable of **reaching** our hearts exactly when we need them. Sometimes it is to bring new joy into our lives, or even new gentleness when we have been hurt by others, in the past. So that we may heal and grow. When someone reaches out for you with their light, don't be afraid. Let them shine their light on you so that you may heal and grow. In time, you will learn to shine your very own light on others who need the same thing.

It is all about paying it forward.

INFINITE YOU

They pass through us in pure moments of **intersection**, when we meet someone just at the right time, who understands where we are right now in this moment with something in our lives. Sometimes, it is because they have recently or right now experienced the same situation in their life, that is causing you pain. In these intersecting moments, you can grow together and through similar lessons in life.

Intersections are beautiful when you learn to recognise the value you bring, while at the same time, the value others bring to you.

Some are to **behold**, to bring comfort in times of suffering, those with gentle, loving and kind hearts, who know just how to hold us both emotionally and physically in our times of deep personal suffering or tragedy. These beautiful people bring the light of love into our lives. Some for a moment and some for a lifetime. Allow the light of love to shine right into your heart. Let it warm your very soul and heal.

In some beautiful moments, people will arrive and **endure** a lifetime by our sides. Honouring us in all that we are and all that we do.

You will never meet these tribe people in your life if you do not get out and do something different. Not only will they bring greatness into your life, but you will equally bring value into theirs. They will surprise you in your low moments in life in ways you never imagined. They will stand applauding your success without apology, and they will be your greatest champions. Sometimes loudly and sometimes quietly whispering, but they have got your back, and nothing feels better when success comes than having the people who stuck with you right there in the light.

To feel into the endurance of pure unconditional love took me the longest to achieve in life. I chased love down like a lioness on a

FIND YOUR TRIBE

hunt. Many of us do the same. The essence of unconditional love does not exist outside us. To find the purest of all loves you must look deep inside yourself and light the flame of self-love within. I liken this to lighting the pilot light in a heater.

Then and only then, will you understand the essence of pure unconditional love. When you learn to radiate unconditional love out into the world, authentically and with humility something magical happens.

I have shared and heard so many delightful stories of TRIBE answering the call in life. I cherish the moments, days, months and years that my TRIBE has served me, and I honour them in my life. It is the continuum of life and our way as humans to unlock our true infinite potential.

> We do, after all, live in an infinite world, so why live finitely?

CHAPTER 13

SHARE YOUR STORY

Be visible, be heard and be awesome because there is someone out there who needs to hear your story and see your light so they can discover their own way.

Just like I am doing with you right now, I cannot overstate how important it is for you to share your story. Every time you open yourself up to being vulnerable and sharing your beautiful story, you give someone else the invitation to do the same. Like snowballs of kindness thrown forward into the world, they will appear in places you never imagined. Sometimes, you will witness the beauty they unfold, but often you will never see the results. Please do not let this stop you from doing it again and again. Together, we will change the world, one beautiful kind act of vulnerability at a time.

It can be hard to share your story, even painful at times, but the simple act of storytelling is a natural human evolutionary skill we all have. Think of our ancestors before there were pens and paper. We didn't have the kind of technology we have now, to connect so quickly and easily, right across the world. Back then, we shared stories by word of mouth, and we passed them down from generation to generation in the simple and yet humble art of conversation.

Your story will be incredibly motivating and powerful for someone to hear. Once you realise this, you will understand that your story is no longer yours to keep. The sharing of your story will enrich your life through connection, in ways you never imagined possible.

Like me, you could become an author and write your story down so that many can read it. Never think that writing a book is beyond your ability because there are many ways to write a book. You can write it yourself or engage a ghostwriter.

Nothing Is beyond your potential other than the ceiling you place above your head.

You can also share your story more intimately with people that you meet. There will be days when you cry and days when you laugh, but the day that someone thanks you for sharing your story because it changed their life forever, will be a day you will never forget.

This outcome is what it looks like when you shine your light so brightly, that as if by magic, illuminating the way for others.

I have had the great joy of sharing my story with many people, as part of the process of writing this book. The connections I made have grown me as a person in ways beyond my wildest dreams, yet I have a feeling it is only just the beginning. I have shared tears of sorrow and tears of joy. I have laughed uncontrollably and delved deep into my suffering, long hidden away to bring my story to life. It has been the most unbelievable journey to date.

SHARE YOUR STORY

The lesson of storytelling is such an important lesson to learn, no matter where you are in life. I will be forever grateful for the opportunity to share my story, as I will be equally grateful always, for the beautiful souls I have met on my journey so far. Life has a way of guiding you well, especially when you take off the armour and step out into the world with vulnerability and courage from within your heart.

A well-known speaker I know once told me of an amazing story that reminded me of how important storytelling is. He spoke of a time where he was addressing a crowd of 10,000 people. When he left the stage, being ushered off to his waiting car to head to the airport home, two people handed him a note each. He was in such a rush that he gave them to his wife, and she put them in her bag without looking at them and they raced to the airport for their flight home.

When they finally got seated on their flight, his wife remembered the two notes and pulled them out of her bag. The first was a remittance for the payment made to him for speaking that day. The second was a note from someone in the audience. It read:

> *"Thank you for speaking. Today I had decided it was going to be my last day as I was going to kill myself, but your story gave me something to live for, so thank you."*

This is the incredible power of your story!

Never forget the power that you hold within you that needs to be shared.

Every time I read this story and hear beautiful stories from others, it fills my heart with such joy knowing that we are changing peoples lives, one moment and one day at a time, simply through that act of sharing our story.

Working as a mindfulness writer and transformation stategist, I have had an amazing life to date, where I get to help ignite peoples passion and co-create the life they desire. It is a privilege that is hard for me to describe in words, but it is one that I am thankful for every day. It is the most humbling privilege to have people come to me, and decide to trust me enough to open their hearts and bare their souls. This is not something I take lightly.

It is my true north, my absolute purpose in life, and I found it tucked away within my very own story.

> Imagine what could be tucked away within your story, to ignite your purpose and full potential!

It is right there for the taking. You have the manual, you might simply need someone to help you find the right pages to look at, but it's all there.

With the right support, you can achieve anything you desire.

This is exciting, don't you think? Through self-expansion, the ripple effect of your growth continues on and on and on. Our expansion is infinite. Go get it! And pay it forward from your heart.

Once I had a client who came to me for the first time, she opened up at the end of the session and said to me, *"Thank you for being the exact person I need at the exact time I needed you."*

SHARE YOUR STORY

This is why I went left when it seemed like everyone was going right in my industry. People told me time and time again, I was mad and I would never be successful in my field unless I followed the crowd, but right at that moment, I felt all the success I needed. For at that moment, I had changed someone's life forever. It is so powerful, and I know it in my heart that we all can do this for others time and time again.

> When you have that feeling in your heart that you know your path is to cut a new one, don't stop and look back!

Just keep moving forward, because when you discover that you are finally cutting a new path, you are most definitely heading in the right direction.

For me, once I started heading in a purposeful direction, it was like someone was standing behind me holding me up. When the obstacles came, I felt it ever so gently guiding me forward, when it was time to move. This feeling gave me a great sense of determination that I knew the way forward, and I just had to trust in the moment and take the opportunities to move when they arrived, one at a time.

There are so many ways to share your story. You can by simply living it, by being genuine and yourself. In this way, you will become a role model for others, giving them the inspiration to do the same. It is simply, the lead by example philosophy that we know all about from places like religious studies at school. You know the 'do unto others as you would like them to do unto you' scenario.

> Live a good life, be free, be kind and be open. That doesn't sound so hard, does it?

Unfortunately, in a world where we rely on external happiness and pleasing others to be liked, it has become more complicated than we would have wanted.

Through my story, I found a way to be the authentic real me. It took hard work and dedication to empty my boxes as you already know. However, in doing so, and sharing my story, I have given many others, the inspiration to be courageous and start that journey for themselves. You don't need to be told it is happening or see it when it starts. I can assure you though it will happen. Keep an eye out on the people around you, and like magic, big things start to happen. I see this happening all the time, not just in my work, but everywhere I have contact with people.

Leading by example is like a beautiful invitation to the best version you could ever want to be. Living the life that you deserve, full of joy. Instead of wishing Friday would arrive every day and dreading Monday when it does. When I say joy, I don't mean this unattainable form of constant happiness either, because we know this simply is only short term. It is the joy of acceptance of what you cannot change, and the joy of changing what you know you can. This is all discoverable and held within your story.

> Can you see how the power of your story is so great to others?

SHARE YOUR STORY

As part of my story, I learned to understand what true sustainable happiness looks like. I would describe sustainable happiness as +2 above the line and -2 below the line. I like to call this the Zone of Contentment. It is pretty much the exact opposite of a +10 sugar hit and -10 come down. It is that consistent feeling of contentment. When things arrive that could potentially annoy you, they don't, and you barely bat an eyelid. Happiness to you then stops being a bouncing Tigger and creates a sense of calmness that tunes into your favourite song right in your heart, all woven within your story.

It is a beautiful feeling to be content, in a world where it seems like things are out of control. Don't get me wrong, this isn't some kind of zen mode of living reserved only for other people. In fact, it is the opposite of what you might think. True contentment accepts all the feelings that arrive and welcomes them with open arms, then you simply decide not to react with fire. This is the powerful way you change your story.

Elizabeth Gilbert says it so delightfully in her book, *Big Magic*. It goes something like this:

> "Anxiety, we are going on a road trip, you can come but under no circumstances can you drive the car."

This is an example of contentment and acceptance of feelings that arise, by not allowing them to control the outcome. We don't have control over what people throw at us, but we most definitely have control of how we respond. The word 'how' is the most important part, because the how shows us that we have options. When you consider your options in the way you respond, sit back and watch how the world around you changes before your very eyes.

INFINITE YOU

This is the next way I discovered how you can change peoples lives by changing your story, and choosing how you tell it to others. It is all in the way you respond. It is a kind of magic to see it in action. It is called flow. When you are in flow, the *how* comes as it needs to, without you forcing a solution.

Here is an example that is familiar to most people. I want you to think of something that you and your partner argue about consistently. You say something, they get annoyed, they say something back, and you get annoyed and boom! We are off and racing once again...

> What would happen if just one of you chose to respond differently, by considering your options before you responded?

> Could this stop the argument from starting at all?

It takes two people to argue, but it only takes one person the change the game by choosing to respond differently, and this is your new story. Maybe, with a gentle and more considered approach, an argument, can be avoided completely.

The first time I took the time to breathe and consider my response, it was a total game-changer. My partner at the time looked at me, then he equally responded differently with a softer and kinder heart. It is like a reflection from a mirror.

SHARE YOUR STORY

If someone throws anger and you mirror it, you get more anger, but if someone throws anger and they get understanding from you, then you are more likely to get understanding back. I have learned the power of the pause and the choice to choose a different response, and it is magical how it transforms relationships one conversation at a time.

> Change your story, tell your story and empower others to do the same. The power is in your hands! What are you going to do with it?

CHAPTER 14

CATCH YOURSELF IN THE ACT

When you can catch yourself in the act of boxing you know you are winning.

When the day arrives and you finally feel like you have tipped all your known boxes – be it one giant one or many out on the floor – you might just discover a few superpowers or even better learn the art of catching yourself in the act of boxing.

> It is that moment when you think, *"I can't deal with this right now!"* where it might actually be time to say, *"Wait a minute. No, don't you even think about it! Why are you putting that in a box?"*

This is magic indeed because you are now ahead of the game. It is time to stop and pat yourself on the back because you have caught yourself in the act of attempted boxing. This is no mean feat. Well done!

INFINITE YOU

For those of you who might not have meditated and considering it, I can tell you it can be incredibly useful.

> I like to call meditation, 'the art of practising to live'.

I'll bet you didn't think of it like that!

Most people think meditation is all about not thinking. It is no wonder that most people don't meditate when they believe, they have to be able to stop thinking completely! The mind is constantly working so the probability of not thinking is very low, especially in the beginning.

Guided meditation usually focuses on your breath. This kind of focused meditation is helpful, so you can catch yourself when your mind drifts off on thoughts. Remember the words, *"Catch yourself."*

Sometimes you can begin to lose focus on your breathing. This can happen in a split second. For instance, you could begin thinking of things in your past. Other times you might daydream about your future. The desire in meditation is to be present, to stay in the here and now, with your breath, one breath at a time.

When you learn to catch your thoughts as they arise in meditation and not get swept away by them, you are practising the same skill as catching yourself in the act of boxing up emotions, pain, suffering and disappointment. The transfer of these skills can be incredibly useful. The correlation is simple yet highly effective in practice.

What you practice in mediation will help you in every area of your life. You will be potentially surprised how quickly you get results

CATCH YOURSELF IN THE ACT

when you start to meditate regularly, even if for only shorts amounts of time every day.

There are many forms of meditation and places you can go to do them. You can attend a meditation class, and you can access meditation apps for your phone to start. The amount of information about basic meditation that is readily available is quite impressive these days. It will get you started in the right direction.

However, I would suggest that when you are ready to progress your meditation to a higher level, you consider getting some guided instruction. This will help to uncover other forms of meditation for consideration as there are many which can be learned, that can enhance all areas of your life.

Don't be fooled meditation isn't just for monks. Ask a monk and they will joyfully share their experience with you. Many amazing forms of meditation can be very rewarding, and help you to find your way, even in the most trying of circumstances. There are meditation meetup groups all over the world, so you are likely to be able to find one somewhere close to your home or online. There is power in proximity, so being around like-minded people who also meditate can bring potential improvement of your individual practice, too.

The trick is to stay aware of your behaviours, so you will always be able to catch yourself in either the act or just about to start a new box. When you manage to catch yourself before you begin to fold out the box, you are most definitely winning. Stay sharp and don't get complacent as these things have a habit of creeping up on you when you least expect them.

When catching myself in the act of boxing up my emotions, suffering and pain, I've found it to be one of the most rewarding practices in life to attain. When self-awareness, combined with focus, is fostered in this way, beautiful things can happen in life.

The courage to be open and honest, breathing life into difficult moments, also when the tough conversations need to be had, is an invaluable skill indeed. One that I am sure you will discover is as rewarding to attain for you as it was on my journey.

Breathe deeply into the moments in your life as they arise, and soon you will discover that they are the only real moments that you have. To understand this is quite profound. The value of developing this practice, in your life, should never be understated. I have helped and supported many people on their meditation journey through my blog and YouTube channel, both called *"The Art of Mindful Disruption"* – the content there is free to use and share with others. I've also had great success in personally coaching clients.

NB: For all my social media channels, refer to the connect with me section at the end of this book. You are welcome to connect and follow me on this journey if you find my work helpful to your expansion.

For it is only in the here and now that you can create the person you want to be tomorrow so that you can attain all that you desire in life. Your ultimate happiness and fulfilment in life are discovered in this moment right now.

> Are you here? Are you feeling it? Whenever you get lost, don't berate yourself. Simply and repetitively come back ever so gently to the NOW. This is a beautiful place where your potential for greatness is infinite, and it is yours to be had.

CHAPTER 15

LIVING ON THE EDGE

Discovering which edge you made home and how to find your way to the middle.

Do you sometimes feel like you are living life on the edge? I am not talking about being a risk-taker and having a dangerous life – I'm actually suggesting that you are standing on a cliff and facing the abyss.

Sometimes we find ourselves on an edge in life metaphorically speaking like this. A place where we did not even realise how we got there. Not to mention that we didn't notice it was an edge until suddenly we began to feel incredibly uncomfortable with the view.

> Has this ever happened to you?

Let me explain the concept of the edge. You see, in my own experience I developed this concept through understanding my own life. We kind of all live on a circle of consciousness. We all have different views that have been developed through years of social and cultural conditioning in life.

This conditioning happens at home, at school, and any other place that you frequent like religious groups and sporting clubs as an example. As we grow we learn about different beliefs, morals & ethical positions. Through this life-long learning, we often attach to one belief, and find ourselves firmly planted on a specific edge with like-minded people. Once this belief becomes rooted in your mindset, you can often no longer see other positions as having validity in your life.

I want you to imagine a circle and almost the entire human race is standing packed shoulder to shoulder, thousands of rows deep, on the edges of that circle looking outwards. They cannot see one another, nor do they realise there is a middle that is almost completely void of people. The reason for this is because they are all facing outwards.

I grew up in a unique family where my mother stood on one edge of what I would now describe as consciousness, and my father on pretty much the exact opposite edge. As a child, I grew up running between these edges and in that space in between is where I discovered the middle was in fact empty. It was like a baron wasteland where virtually no-one was looking inwards. Take this a step further and we actually replicate this in ourselves individually. We seek everything external to us, just like humanity seeks all the answers externally on the circle of consciousness.

So, by now you have probably realised that the edge in this circle of consciousness is simply a position taken by a person based on their belief system. My mum identified among many things as an Atheist, while my father was a firm believer of God. There are many reasons why my parents developed their beliefs. It is important to note that none are right or wrong, they are all simply positions taken up in our minds, through generations of conditioning passed down from parent to child over thousands of years.

The beautiful thing is that at anytime you can change your position simply by changing your beliefs.

As a young child, it is perfectly normal for you to desire to please both your parents and have their love and support in your life. This, however, becomes complicated when you grow up in a space with completely conflicting views on religion, or any other belief really. Whether it's healthy eating, religion, race, science, spirituality, sport or sexuality beliefs, these are imprints that have been overlaid on you from birth. Some by force and some so subtle that you hardly recognise their existence, creating generational bias.

I spent more than 40 years of my life conflicted by my parent's views on religion. I ran back and forth from edge to edge, feeling like I had to pick a side to be on, like a team. Eventually, as a teenager, I gave in and picked a side out of pressure. As I matured and gained valuable life experience and insight, I started to discover that maybe I had made an error of judgement. That it is quite possible that I didn't need to pick a side at all.

> I began to ask myself, *"Why can't I be in the middle and accept the positions of all the beliefs that exist?"*

In my teenage years and through into my 20s, I read about many religions, cultures and ethical belief systems. In doing this, I realised that there were more commonalities than differences which surprised me, because I certainly didn't get this perspective from any other source in life. It is my belief that the same can be applied for all of humanity. If only we saw the things that make us the same rather than the things that make us different, I believe that humanity would be in a much better position.

Instead, we divide and conquer, focused almost completely on what makes us different. From sex, sexuality, religion, politics, race and beliefs, we have drawn strong lines of division in the proverbial sand, holding strong at these lines like a battleground, defending our position as if it was a personal matter of honour – while the basis of humanity remains exactly the same.

> So, why do we do this?

There are many positions taken as to why we choose to align within smaller groups that we somehow have chosen to identify with. These positions are not always driven by malice, but much more subtle and often difficult to identify on the surface. The best way to articulate the subtlety of where this can occur in life is through a personal example.

Once I moved from one state to another in Australia. The state I moved to was significantly more multicultural than the one I left. I was single and I dated a number of men of different cultures to me. I see people as people, before I see their cultures, beliefs or nationalities.

Equally, I am often intrigued by other cultures and so the conversations I find are interesting with new people of different cultures whether it is in my work, interests or dating.

LIVING ON THE EDGE

In a very non deliberate or judgemental way, a friend I left behind in the previous state brought this to my attention. She said that she had realised that she had been brought up by a strong white bias, as she didn't think she would likely date someone of another non-white culture. The discovery of this surprised her as she didn't see herself as racist at all and neither did I for that matter. This is the subtlety of cultural bias. It exists in every part of the world, yet when you begin to look below the surface, it is fairly easy to recognise it within yourself.

So, today I simply suggest for you to come and check out the middle. This is where I have personally found acceptance, understanding and contentment. I discovered a space of infinite possibilities, truths and liberation of social conditioning.

It is a place I describe as the 'middle in the circle of consciousness'.

For now, consider this. In the middle, it is quiet, allowing time for contemplation and reflection. If you can bravely take a step back from the over crowded edge you have found yourself on, come into the middle, even for a little while, and experience some peace and quiet. You might be surprised as to what you can learn about both yourself and the world in which you live and breathe. Then, the more of us who do this, the greater the opportunity for signifiant change in this beautiful world that we all call home.

I leave you with the idea to ponder, that the middle indeed might just hold the key to elevated consciousness, and a beautiful reigniting of the flame of humanity that is burning ever so gently within us all. Hidden in plain sight, behind all our backs. All you need to do is turn around and take a look for yourself.

INFINITE YOU

> What have you got to lose?

> Is it possible that the future of humanity is relying on us to do this important work so that we can move forward as the collective sum of our parts? Rather than race to the finish line, fighting and competing for an unknown prize?

> What if there is enough for us all?

When you learn to first understand where you stand in the circle of consciousness, you discover two incredibly important things. You belong to something much bigger than you ever imagined possible, as you realise that there is no glue holding you were you are, except the thoughts that are trapping you in your head.

Let your heart lead you forward, one step, one moment, one person at a time. When you find others in the centre of the 'circle of consciousness', they will welcome you here, and you will have shown the way forward for every person who you have touched in your journey into the 'middle'.

Come join me and discover the fine art of contentment versus the roller-coaster ride you are likely on in life called stress. The middle of the circle of consciousness is warm, filled with love, forgiveness, kindness, humility and hope.

We are waiting for you to arrive.

CHAPTER 16

THE CURVE OF CONTENTMENT

*Discovering the fine art of contentment
versus the roller-coaster ride of stress.*

In the fast-paced world we live in, stress is at an all-time high. We are on a trajectory for collapse. I have already alluded to the concept of contentment as I learned it myself. It may seem like a heavy concept but in this chapter, I will show you how I discovered a way forward of which it's simplicity might surprise you.

The world that we are living in has vastly changed with the pandemic taking the world, as it would seem, by storm. The stress that many of us saw and experienced was already at crazy levels. This so often continued to rise due to financial and personal circumstances impacting us all. But, when you begin to look at it through a different lens, you will discover that some equally amazing things also happened throughout the pandemic.

People began to question what was important in their lives in ways many have never before. For many, the world was tipped on its head, and will forever be changed. Change, even though it may be scary, is quite a marvellous thing indeed. I have always been one of those people who thrive through change and disruption. It is a skill, however most definitely one that can be learned, like all things in life. One firstly needs to have the desire to learn and a teacher to provide the learning space.

Through many years of yoga and meditation practice, I have learned not to get attached grabbing onto a tree, as I float down the river of life. Life itself it would seem is what causes the stress. Yet in all reality, It is merely the attachment and identification of situations on the way that cause our stress. As Buddha says, *"You cannot control what happens to you, but you can control how you react."*

Understanding the curve of contentment helps to see the benefits and the possibilities in life that can be achieved, by reducing the need to be a perfect 10.

> Wouldn't that be nice?

> Imagine a world where you didn't feel pressured to be perfect.

For perfection is the unattainable dream, that so many of us, have been trapped in for a lifetime. Sometimes it is our very own undoing, and for others it is the desire to be liked. However, frequently it is a mix of both.

As Squire Bill Wildener once said, "Do what you can, from where you are, with what you have."

THE CURVE OF CONTENTMENT

I humbly agree – as did Theordore Roosevelt. When you begin to think this way, you are always enough. It is a simple philosophy but not as easy to achieve as one might think. This is because of the impact of social and cultural conditioning. We are, unfortunately through no fault of our own, conditioned to consistently compete, compare, and strive for perfection.

We are taught throughout our entire life that in a rating out of 10, while 10 is the best, one is the worst. It is the scorecard of life and all that it entails. From the beginning throughout our school education all the way through to our working lives, and everything else in-between. We are all striving for the perfect 10. But it doesn't exist, perfection that is. It is simply the obstacle that most commonly, you put in your way to cause yourself endless suffering in life.

> Why do we get in our own way? Why do we cause ourselves so much suffering unnecessarily you might say? It is an important question to consider. However, the answer might surprise you.

We do it so instinctively that we don't even realise we are doing it most of the time. Our conditioning over time is overlaid with stories, that create automated responses each time the opportunity comes up to validate and keep score.

If you look around your life, you will notice there is an underlying current of judgement that exists everywhere, and perfectionism is simply a symptom of judgement. This might feel like a bitter pill to swallow, however, if you honestly look deeper into your perfectionism as I had to myself. You will find that judgement runs deep, and it is usually fuelled by fear. It is like a toxic cocktail in your subconscious, that creates fires again and again and again.

> So, what does contentment look like?

Before we go there, we really need to take a side step and look at what perfection causes. The #1 output of perfectionism is stress. All that striving is going to takes its toll, after all.

> Did you know that stress is the #1 cause of premature death?

This is easy to understand when we consider the concept of disease. Which, when you break it down, is dis-ease – meaning the lack of ease within the body. It is commonly and widely accepted now that when we stress the body, at some point things go wrong.

You don't need to be a doctor or scientist to undertand this. Yet it is preventable in almost every circumstance – if you get it under control when it's stress, before it become disease. Our society is riddled with stress from a young age. As an adult, we'll even wear it like a badge of honour. That is until it stops us dead in our tracks – and that is if it doesn't actually kill us first. For many, it does just that. Stress triggers anxiety and underlying issues in life that have been left unattended and unresolved, opening old wounds and creating new ones in the process.

> So, why have we almost entirely become a society that is championing the cause of stress, like an honourable status symbol?

THE CURVE OF CONTENTMENT

We seem to have decided that it is a necessary evil. We know through science that once we accept something that we think we cannot change, all we then do is create a whole bunch of coping mechanisms to deal with it day-to-day. The real problem drifts below the surface of the water. Like a giant iceberg barely seeing the small bit above the surface; while below the surface, a giant problem is hidden from view, masked by drugs, alcohol, sugar, coffee, over-eating, resentment, retreat, submission, anger, and a plethora of defensive behaviours. All this enacted to somehow protect ourselves, yet the damages continues to be done out of sight and out of mind.

In the wash up, we have seen suicide increase exponentially along with a whole host of mental health problems in a society that is on a fast roller-coaster ride to nowhere any of us want to go.

> Don't you think it might be time to apply the brakes?

If we managed businesses the way we managed stress in our society, there would be no businesses left to count. In business, we have risk management strategies, root cause analysis and a whole load of other methodologies and strategies to get to the root cause of problems to save money and time. Yet we bury stress within ourselves quicker than the blink of an eye.

> Why?

Social and cultural conditioning, that's why. Because generations of conditioning has been applied and now we literally accept stress like it is the norm.

> So, what if I told you that there was a better way?

That, if you aimed for a 5, instead of a 10, you would drastically reduce your risk factors associated with stress and the disease that comes with it. It's a surprise to most people I share this idea with. However, the higher above five you go, the lower below five you will go when things are not going your way. So, if you are hell-bent on having level 10 energy and achieving a 10 score in everything you do, you will equally have extreme lows, as well.

This is what is known as the yo-yo effect of an energy timeline. Extremes become incredibly hard to manage, and this is where stimulants come into play.

> We know them all well, namely caffeine and sugar to manage the energy lows. The decline only gets steeper from here on out, if you miss the signs.

I like the Dalai Lama's description of it in one of his books, where he talks about it as the well of life. We spend our entire life going up and down the rope in the well. Sometimes we are at the top, and sometimes rock bottom and no one wants to be at rock bottom for long. But the truth is more people are there more often than necessary, and it all comes back to the perfection dilemma, driven by the judgement race car, with the main driver being fear.

> To learn how to develop a life of contentment takes both unlearning old habits and a willingness to learn new ones.

THE CURVE OF CONTENTMENT

Along with learning to understand individually what drives your personal contentment, it's critically important to understand that contentment is not being disinterested or disengaging in your work or life. It is about realising that it is impossible to strive for a 10 non-stop in life. It is time to pick your battles.

It is not a one shoe fits all approach, because we are all unique. One thing I am certain of is that it's not only possible for anyone to find contentment, but it's equally possible to learn how to maintain it in any storm.

It is not strange nor impossible, but through the adoption of an infinite mindset, it is possible to escape the trappings of the world, causing you to be stuck in that well going up and down for what seems like all eternity. The irony here is that once you escape the drive for perfection you learn to understand that there are no limits to what you can achieve. Perfection merely stops you from making mistakes, which are vital to experience infinite potential.

> Instead of being wound up like a spring and having no patience, would you like a more content life? One where when things go wrong, you don't completely flip your lid? How about a world where you are not expected to be jumping out of your skin happy, every waking moment? Does that sound like a much more doable thing to achieve?

I know this one well because I backed myself completely into the corner of perfectionism, and high energy very early in life. I chased everything down like a crazy woman and I stopped for no-one. I got all the warning signs, all throughout my life. This included anxiety as a child which lead into deeper anxiety as an adult, and stress that finally lead to illness. After years of ignoring all the signs, I finally hit the wall, and had a complete meltdown. It wasn't pretty at all; they never are.

Today, I know and understand that a meltdown was always coming for me, because I ignored all the mini meltdowns on the way. I have reflected much on my life, however today I choose to listen to my body and observe my actions in the present moment.

I am incredibly grateful that my wakeup call in life didn't have to come by way of a severe illness. The fact that my health I had lost was able to be returned with effort, and an acceptance that I needed to change everything, was a remarkable gift.

> Like me, you can step out of the corner you've backed yourself into at any time, as you too have that off switch – which you can hit at literally any time you like.

The curve of contentment concept simply suggests considering the potential for maintaining a more reliable and comfortable energy timeline. You see, in life, we were simply not designed to maintain high energy all the time. Just as the day changes from day into night, we are designed to rest. Statistically, on average, we are not getting the rest we need either in relaxation or sleep.

Our diets are full of stimulants to keep us awake, and commonly, we are using sleeping pills to reverse this process at night. Cortisol levels are over heightened, and quality sleep is highly under-valued, causing us no end of physiological and phycological problems, as we face a constant everchanging world.

THE CURVE OF CONTENTMENT

When you learn to manage your energy timeline closer to a five, sudden change is going to have less impact, and your energy usage is far more moderate. This allows for moments of heightened energy, rather than trying to sustain unrealistic energy outputs.

Some of you might be thinking, well, I'm a naturally high energy person. My suggestion is to take away the stimulants and have another look. You might be surprised, as I was, with what you discover. Caffeine, sugar and the plethora of other stimulants in mainstream lifestyles have created a false presence of energy that is not naturally sustainable.

If you would like to truly have a life of joy encapsulating more realistic expectations including acceptance – and avoid the #1 killer of stress – then it might be time to reevaluate your perception of perfection, driven by the race car of judgement, fueled by fear.

Before I leave you to contemplate the concept of contentment in your life, it's important that you understand contentment is not a boring life. This belief is formed on the backbone of your social and cultural conditioning.

> Contentment is a deep sense of joy that comes from within your heart.

It feels beautiful, natural and nurturing to rediscover it and bring it forward into your life. Contentment means living a life without stress, anxiety and to hop off the roller coaster ride of perfection.

Choose today to start.

CHAPTER 17

INFINITE YOU

Begin as you wish to continue.

Many years ago, a friend of mine was getting married. Her father shared a piece of advice with us on her wedding day. I can't remember the exact words, but today I recall it as, *"Begin as you wish to continue."*

I was in my early 20s, and I had absolutely no idea what he meant or in fact, how profound these words would become for me 20 years later in life. It was a piece of gold that he shared, and in the many years that followed, I learned to appreciate it through experience.

> You are probably thinking the same as I did at the time. What does it mean - begin as you wish to continue?

It sounded to me like he was speaking in code or riddles like you think adults do when you are young. At the time, I most likely parked the idea, somewhere within the filing system of my mind.

INFINITE YOU

In simplified terms, beginning as you wish to continue can simply mean that the decisions you make about how you live today will impact your tomorrow. As a person in my early 20s, I didn't catch this at all.

When we're young, there is so much coming at us, especially today in the technology era of hyperdrive information at our fingertips.

The world has changed a lot since I was 20, and this is a completely natural phenomenon know as forward motion in time. We know that life changes, and with these changes, I too changed and therefore, eventually became able to understand what my friend's father actually meant.

> So, if you want tomorrow to be different than today, then you need to do the work today to make it happen. Or else you will get to tomorrow and think why am I still stuck here? Or how did I get here at all?

It can also mean to be your true self from the beginning of every relationship. Authenticity is essential for living an infinite life. It may have taken me 20 years to fully understand the depth of what this means, however, the learning on the way to understanding has been invaluable, and I would not have wanted it any other way. You see, when I asked my friends dad what he meant he said something like, *"Life will teach you."*

He was certainly right there.

Through life experience, I discovered that if I changed myself to impress someone else or make them happy, one day, I eventually got tired of the facade. It would culminate in me suddenly and desperately wanting to be me. This is problematic, causing confusion and surprise that suddenly, out of what seems like nowhere at all, you are different.

At first, I wished I had understood this concept or that maybe it was explained to me when I was in my 20s – it may have been particularly useful when I was facing the reality of divorce by 26. However, in reflection, quite possibly it was a poignant life lesson to learn. To understand for yourself instead of being shown, can help you grow much further in life.

> For understanding yourself is likely one of the most important and valuable lessons in life you are likely to learn.

The reality is, at 21, I was probably not in a place to understand. However, what I think he actually did was something quite beautiful. He had lovingly planted a seed and was happy to just let it be.

When you plant a seed, you are not always the person who waters it or sees it grow.

Sometimes, you are just the seed planter. When the time is right, the waterer and nurturer come along to ripen the idea, which may quite possibly support the bearing of fruit in your life. How lovely is it that my friend's father dished it up at such a pivotal time in his daughter's life, the beginning of her marriage? I often wonder if she heeded the advice.

These beautiful words got buried in a box, which I discovered when I went on my journey of unpacking my life. It is a journey that never really ends. Sometimes, life just weaves and winds like a delightful country lane, and other times, it feels as though you are stuck in hyperdrive rushing from place to place.

Remember once you have learned and put into practice the steps to unbox the suffering, regret, sorrow and disappointment from your past, these skills will remain there for you always. Feeling lighter having released the things that held you back and regathering the parts of you, that you left behind.

On your forward journey, put your feet down each day, one step at a time, on the journey of life. Remembering always that life is a journey, not a destination. Enjoy the journey, be brave, be vulnerable and keep unpacking those boxes as they become visible to you.

Use these tools wisely and you will have a life full of joy, regret and sorrow – in fact, all of the emotions because they are all part of life as a human. Enjoy them all unboxed, spilled out on the floor, raw and completely you just as you were meant to be. Someone is waiting for you to show up as the authentic you.

> What are you waiting for?

You have all you need. Now, you just need to find that safe space, where you can get going and unpacking your boxes for a lighter and brighter road ahead!

Remember this:

> *"With an infinite mindset, there is no winning or losing, just ahead and behind."* (Simon Sinek)

INFINITE YOU

Sometimes in life, you are ahead and sometimes, you are behind, but your actions will determine if you stay there or if you move forward.

With an infinite mindset, your potential is limitless; as are your options.

Awareness helps you to see these as they arrive in your life. In life, to see the infinite potential that lays before you, you'll need to learn to stop forcing solutions with your finite mindset.

Instead, try creating an intention, being the end game you want to achieve. Apply attention to your intention, which looks more like awareness. Then and only then will you be open to the infinite opportunities that exist all around you in every situation.

Stop setting the bar so low with a finite mindset, allow the bar to raise naturally and live an infinite life, filled with wonder and joy that you were always meant to live.

I learned to raise the bar not by force but by intention. Today, I live a beautiful life, practicing the embodiment of love, one person, one situation and one moment at a time.

As the infamous Buzz Lightyear once said,*"To infinity and beyond!"*

ABOUT THE AUTHOR
∞

Jeanette was born in the UK and moved to Australia as a young child. She has over 25 years of experience as a professional business woman who brings a well overdue new meaning to the idea of a modern day yogi, speaker, mindfulness writer and transformation strategist, while openly sharing her wisdom of love and life.

Her experience spans running her own businesses, project management and consulting in the corporate space, working in disability services, not for profit organisations, retail, hospitality, contact centres, education, IT and technology innovation. She is a game changer, determined to create a better world to leave behind.

Jeanette is passionate about rising to all occasions to become the very best version of herself, so she can help others tap into their authenticity and discover their infinite potential.

She writes this book in the hope that it will inspire you to share your story, grow to be your best version of you each and every day, and help others to do the same through the magic of the ripple effect.

ACKNOWLEDGEMENTS

∞

I wish to thank the beautiful people in my life who read parts of my book during the writing process. Your feedback was invaluable and your support of my work much appreciated.

I wish to thank the Australian photographer, David Nightingale, for the amazing image on the cover of this book. His photography is incredible as is his zest for life.

I wish to acknowledge the beautiful Inram Abul Kashem for the photo supplied of me. He is not only a great personal photographer but also a divine human being who I am grateful to have had the pleasure to cross paths with in life.

I wish to acknowledge the amazing and beautiful people that have traversed my life. Some of whom stayed and some whom have moved on. Your love and your lessons in life were invaluable and for that, I will always be grateful.

CONNECT WITH ME

∞

If you would like to:

- follow me on social media
- read my articles
- listen to my YouTube channel
- order a book for a friend

visit my website or scan the QR code below.

https://www.mindfuldisruption.com.au

REFLECTIONS
∞

INFINITE YOU

REFLECTIONS

INFINITE YOU

REFLECTIONS

www.ingramcontent.com/pod-product-compliance
Lightning Source LLC
Chambersburg PA
CBHW041142110526
44590CB00027B/4096